THE POWER OF PERSONAL ACCOUNTABILITY
Achieve What Matters to You

by Mark Samuel and Sophie Chiche

What people are saying about The Power of Personal Accountability:

KEN BLANCHARD / Coauthor, *The One Minute Manager*® and *The Leadership Pill*™

"*The Power of Personal Accountability: Achieve What Matters to You* is an inspirational and practical guide for self-improvement. I recommend it to anyone who wants to become the CEO of his or her own life."

ERNIE BANKS / "Mr. Cub" — Baseball Hall of Famer, 512 Career Home Run Hitter

"I played for one remarkable team and for one great city almost of my baseball career and I have been so blessed. What can I say about this inspirational book? It supports what I've always believed: The commitments we make and keep to ourselves and the people in our lives are the key to achieving our genuine dreams."

ARIANNA HUFFINGTON / Syndicated Columnist, Author of *Fanatics and Fools*

"*The Power of Personal Accountability: Achieve What Matters To You* is an inspiring and much-needed guide to being accountable in work, at home, in relationships, and in all aspects of life. Mark Samuel and Sophie Chiche have written a practical and common-sense book that can help people in all walks of life reclaim power over their lives and achieve their goals."

ELIZABETH FORSYTHE HAILEY / Author, *A Woman of Independent Means*

"An empowering book that provides tough-minded strategics for avoiding the trap of victimhood and becoming the hero of your own life."

LARRY M. ZUCKER, L.C.S.W.

"As a marriage counselor and family therapist, I've found that when people try to be accountable, that is, try to account to each other for the complicated or conflictual experience they are sharing, things get better. Yet when they confuse accountability with blame, things get rapidly worse. Mark Samuel and Sophie Chiche masterfully clear up this confusion, and draw many interesting maps for being accountable in a range of relational contexts, from the interpersonal on up to the corporate workplace."

DR. MARY E.F. McINERNEY, PH.D. / Principal, The Richard H. Hungerford School, NYC Department of Education, Special Education

"In an accountable environment, the incentive to learn and excel comes from the inside. Mark and Sophie's book challenges us to take an honest look at our own level of personal accountability and how it has created both our individual and communal environments. *The Power of Personal Accountability* engages, heartens, and directs the reader—I highly recommend it."

JAMES T. LUSSIER / President / CEO, St. Charles Medical Center, Oregon

"Creating a comprehensive healing environment for our patients and their families is critical to every aspect of our mission of service. That can only be achieved by first creating a positive, supportive, and healing environment for our caregivers, our employees. We have come to appreciate how essential and powerful the concept of personal accountability really is and have incorporated the methods taught in this book for over eight years. I believe it is key to any transformational leader who wants to move his or her organization to new levels of sustainable excellence."

LIEUTENANT DAVID KAIN / New York City Fire Department, Retired

"A fire officer lives and breathes accountability to his superiors, the men under his command that dare to go with him into the most dangerous situations, and his community. Most of all, he is accountable to himself for his decisions. Without accountability, there is no fire service. Let this book be an inspiration and direction for you to move forward in your life bravely and purposefully."

KIRK FROGGATT / Vice President and Organization Development, Agilent Technologies, Inc.

"As human beings, we are blessed with the gift of conscious thought and choice. In *The Power of Personal Accountability*, Mark and Sophie distinguish the victim loop from the accountability loop and help us see how we can choose our attitudes and actions, even when the situation feels out of our control. This freedom of choice is the Holy Grail—the source of fulfillment and success for all of us, personally as well as professionally."

JAMES W. MONTGOMERY / Retired Bishop, Episcopal Diocese of Chicago

"All cultures, colors, and faiths create the mosaic of our community. Our character and calling are best shared with our community by expressing our heart through action. *The Power of Personal Accountability* is an extraordinary book that gives us a road map for bringing forward our unique selves in a way that supports ourselves and the community we live in."

DAVID WILLIAMS / Executive Vice President / COO, Habitat for Humanity International

"Eliminating poverty housing and homelessness from the world, and making decent shelter a matter of conscience and action requires all aspects of society to exemplify the highest levels of personal accountability. Whether building a house, a community, or one's own life of fulfillment, this book guides the reader to actualizing his or her most sincere dreams."

OLIVIA, thirteen years old

"Mom and Dad have read this book about accountability. I am not sure I really know what that means but I know it is cool that now, they do what they say they are going to do."

DR. BRIAN POSTL / President and CEO, Winnipeg Regional Health Authority; Appointed Member, National Health Council of Canada

"Mark Samuel has the capacity to transform healthcare systems. In a culture where we can never achieve enough on behalf of patients nor can we have sufficient resources to meet all needs, we can be frequently overwhelmed. The capacity to convert health workers from victims to accountable professionals is a key need. It is through this renewed sense of accountability, to our patients and to each other, that healthcare will achieve its rightful place as an outstanding industry."

HEIDE BANKS / Author / Representative to the UN on behalf of the Center for Partnership Studies

"This book provides an undeniable road map taking readers on a journey from victim to champion in their own lives. An essential educating tool for parents, partners, and leaders alike."

PAUL TRINIDAD / Operations Manager, Vistakon, Johnson & Johnson VISION PRODUCTS, Inc.

"I researched for years looking for a simple way of describing accountability without all the negative stuff associated with it. The Personal Accountability Model is the answer. This method has assisted my staff and our employees to move away from resistance, blame, or hiding, and to learn how to take full accountability for the success of their actions. As a result, we are more successful than ever."

RABBI LEVI MEIER, PH.D. / Chaplain, Cedars-Sinai Medical Center, Los Angeles, CA; Clinical Psychologist in Private Practice; Author, *Ancient Secrets*

"I really liked this book. It is an easy-to-read, extremely clear guide to taking responsibility for yourself and where you want to go in life. If you feel that your life is directed by external events and forces, this work will show you how to harness your own unique power and achieve a happier, fuller life."

ADAM CLARK / Age 19, Los Angeles, CA

"Growing up doesn't mean being perfect. I realize it's better for me to take responsibility for myself rather than try to get away with something. Parents can be tough, but the more I take responsibility for my life, the more my parents trust me and let me be independent. I learned a lot about being accountable from this book, *The Power of Personal Accountability*. It's pretty cool."

DR. JOHN W. McCREDIE / Chief Information Officer, Associate Vice Chancellor–Information Technology, University of California, Berkeley

"Providing effective IT solutions to a large research university populated with current and future leaders requires the highest level of customer service and performance execution. At the heart of being effective is the core value of accountability. We have used the strategies and skills taught in this book to turn the value of accountability into an operational reality. As a result, employee morale and customer satisfaction have measurably, consistently, and substantially improved in our organization over the past six years."

ANTHONY E. SHAW / Vice President, Human Resources, North America, DHL Danzas Air and Ocean

"This is a powerful and necessary book. It is a dynamic guide to deconstructing the self-imposed cycle of living with the blinders of feeling victimized and to building self-actualized, productive, and fulfilling lives. There can be no greater personal triumph and no more profound change in the way in which we work."

JOSEPH P. ALLEN / President, National Technology Transfer Center

"Creating an accountable organization is a great challenge for any leader. Using the strategies described in this book, we reached a level of productivity we could only have imagined previously. Just as importantly, our morale is much higher as well."

TERRY TILLMAN / Author, *The Writings on the Wall*

"After reading the first sentences, I wanted to read more: 'It's about what gets you up in the morning. It's about looking back at your life and liking what you see.' This book makes big promises about the powerful life results possible through accountability—and it delivers. Mark and Sophie clearly, and with great examples, present practical strategies, keys, and tools for the fulfillment of your life dreams. They are on to something fundamental and essential with their focus on accountability. This book is a winner!"

STU SEMIGRAN / President and Co-Founder, EduCare Foundation

"Our mission is to teach our youth the three new R's: Respect, Resiliency, and Responsibility. An underlying value for achieving this end is personal accountability. The concepts and methods taught in this book are practical and valuable for teenagers and anyone guiding teenagers to become future leaders and responsible citizens."

ROBERT J. BYERTS, JR. / Supervisory Deputy, United States Marshals Service

"In my line of business, personal accountability is a matter of life and death. The underlying driving force of every initiative, every mission, is our accountability to the people of this country and to the law we uphold. Mark Samuel and Sophie Chiche go directly to the core of this issue, while providing a clear and powerful action plan for success."

DR. H. RONALD HULNICK / President, University of Santa Monica

"Here at the University of Santa Monica it is essential that we provide a sacred and supportive educational environment within which each student can achieve significant and lasting personal and professional goals. I am pleased to see that Mark and Sophie have put the principles and keys to paper that Mark has been using with our staff over the past five years to assist us in attaining and maintaining a high level of accountability."

DR. ROBERT L. BARBER / President, Central Oregon Community College

"Colleges as learning communities are environments where students and staff mutually hold each other accountable to experience personal, academic, and professional growth. *The Power of Personal Accountability* provides a practical and understandable approach to taking one's education and applying it to everyday challenges, the achievement of personal goals, and ultimately a productive life."

GENE D. THIN ELK / CEO, Medicine Wheel, Inc., Red Road Teachings

"This book, *The Power of Personal Accountability*, goes beyond feel good concepts. There are common-sense gems of applications intertwined with appropriate knowledge information to form wisdom transition points for healing. It is transformative, powerful, and practical."

CELIA ROCKS / Author, *Brilliance Marketing* and *101 Publishing Tips for Speakers and Consultants*

"What a wonderful, life-changing book! What Mark and Sophie have done is to create a guide for getting everything you want in a way that helps others, too. Creating a life culture of accountability is the best way to discover true success."

PERRY J. LUDY / Author, *Profit Building, Cutting Costs Without Cutting People*

"*The Power of Personal Accountability* is a meal served up nicely for corporations, and individuals who have an appetite for achieving results. Each page offers valuable insight and how-to in order to help us get started toward achieving what truly matters. Additionally, the authors identify a major hurdle that we all face , but show us how to quickly eliminate it through the powerful gift of forgiveness. Accountability starts with a first step."

VIC PARRISH / Chief Executive Officer / Chief Nuclear Officer, Energy Northwest

"I have always had a personal dedication to accountability. Managing a nuclear energy facility, I can't think of a more essential core value to our success, than accountability. This book delivers a powerful model for leaders and for those who want to change their life to be more purposeful and successful."

DAVID ALLEN / Author, *Getting Things Done: The Art of Stress-Free Productivity* and *Ready for Anything: 52 Productivity Principles for Work and Life*

"Sophie and Mark have produced a terrific operations manual for getting and staying in the driver's seat of life. It's an ever-valuable reminder that no matter where we find ourselves, in a moment's notice we can get positively engaged in where we want to go."

CHRISTINA R. CAMPBELL / Christina Campbell & Company / Supercuts

"Supercuts is dedicated to customer service and providing high quality services and products. Yet, customer expectations are increasing each year. Exceeding customer expectations can only happen with each employee's commitment to personal accountability, where they evolve to higher levels of performance and communication to meet those needs. *The Power of Personal Accountability* has provided our team with the inspiration and tools to make those improvements so we can continually raise the bar on customer service."

LORAL LANGEMEIER / President, Founder, Live Out Loud

"The first step to creating a wealthy life is starting from wherever you are today. That self-honesty takes the highest level of personal accountability. Mark and Sophie's book assists us in moving past the judgments that often keep us stuck in limitation, freeing us to experience a life of prosperity and abundance."

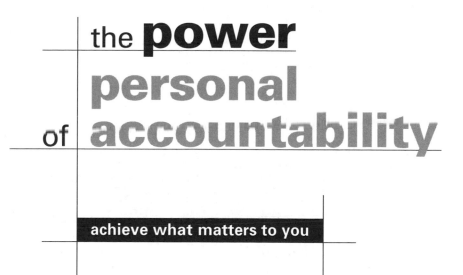

the power of personal accountability

achieve what matters to you

Mark Samuel and Sophie Chiche

XEPHOR
PRESS

XEPHOR
P R E S S

Xephor Press
3 Holly Hill Lane
Katonah, NY 10536
www.xephorpress.com
914-232-6708

First printing

Hardcover: ISBN 0-9752638-2-X
Paperback: ISBN 978-0-9752638-1-5

Printed and bound in the United States of America.

To Leah
To Sarah

To Danny
To Nancy

In memory of Barbara Novak

TABLE OF CONTENTS

This book includes stories about both Sophie Chiche and Mark Samuel. Please note that these personal accounts and experiences are written as a singular "voice of the author" and are written in the first person.

INTRODUCTION

This is a book about accomplishing what matters to you. It is about what gets you up in the morning. It is about looking back at your life and liking what you see. Liking how you handled your family and your career. Liking the reputation you gained with people you worked with and for, how you treated your friends and yourself. Liking how you contributed to your community. It is about liking the difference you made. With your time and money. With your health and spiritual quest. With your talents and professional skills. For you to like what you see when you look back, are you doing the best you can right now?

This is a book about not waiting until the end of your life to deliberately select what is in it. It is about choosing as you go. Every decision you make. Every interaction you have at your office or with your kids. Or yourself. Every moment of every day.

I remember visiting my uncle Philip in a nursing home, years ago. I was told he wasn't ready to see me and was sent to the park to wait for him. A man who introduced himself as Bob was sitting on a bench there and we started a conversation. He was wearing a straw hat to protect himself from a glaring sun. He probably never knew how much he affected me. He had married a young girl he barely knew when he was nineteen. He never really liked her. He lived in the suburbs of Chicago and that never felt like home. He had been an engineer and never liked that either. His kids lived far away, and he rarely saw them. He wasn't complaining about any of it. He wasn't angry. He wasn't sad.

He just described it in a monotone voice. I am not sure he knew he could have had a different life.

I am not sure he knew he had any power over his circumstances and he lived his life by default. His peacefulness seemed to come from a certain resignation. It was the deck he was dealt, and that was the life he had. My uncle came and I said good-bye to Bob. When I came to visit my uncle again a month later, I asked about Bob. He had died a week after our meeting.

His words leaked into my psyche and are behind many of my decisions. When I am at the end of my life sitting on a bench somewhere wearing a straw hat to protect myself from a glaring sun, and someone sits next to me, I want to say that I loved my life. I want to talk about that lunch I shared with my children—how we were laughing so much we could hardly eat. I want to say that I held my friend Joan's hand as cancer was taking her life. I want to talk about the award I won for best customer service when I was starting my career. I want to say that I moved to another country to pursue my spiritual quest. Sitting on that bench, I want to say that I left a comfortable relationship to be alone when I knew I wouldn't find happiness in it. I pursued each job with excellence and a clear intention to support my coworkers and the firms I worked for. And when I was in a job I didn't like, I did everything I could to either change it or find ways to appreciate the one I had. I started rollerblading in my thirties, playing guitar and painting in my forties, and sitting on that bench, I want to be thinking of learning Italian. I lived a full life. I filled it with what mattered to me.

And that is what this book is about. A deliberate life. An accountable life.

Change Your Glasses

For a moment, please forget everything you know about accountability. Forget blaming and finger pointing. Forget "who is responsible for this mistake?" Forget the definitions you've heard, the conversations you've had, the conflicts you're holding on to. Erase everything and start with a clean slate.

Accountability is doing what we say we are going to do.

How else can we accomplish what matters to us?

"At the heart of being accountable is the matter of caring," Max DePree wrote in *Leadership Is an Art*. DePree, then chairman and CEO of Herman Miller, Inc., said accountability was "the right of all working people." It's the way to fulfillment, professional and personal.

Success and accountability go together. Happiness and accountability go together.

Freedom and accountability go together.

I am inviting you throughout this book to visit the world of accountability.

With new eyes. With an open mind.

Victim vs. Accountable

This book is built around The Personal Accountability Model. It was created in 1986 when I was consulting with an executive team. They described a situation in which everybody seemed stuck and unable to perform due to a massive dose of victimhood. I drew this model on a board to describe what I was hearing and other options that could lead to more success.

The model starts when a situation comes up—and it's usually a challenging one. Based on your *intention*, you have a *choice* regarding how to respond. When you take the victim road, you *ignore* the problem, *deny* your involvement in it, and eventually *blame* someone else. Then, you *rationalize* and justify why another person should take care of it and *resist* any attempt that others may make to get you involved. Finally, you *hide* to avoid dealing with it.

Given the same situation, based on an intention to *stay accountable*, you make a different choice. You *recognize* the problem and take *ownership* for getting it resolved. You *forgive* yourself and others who may have contributed to the problem. You are then in the position to *self-examine* how you contributed to the problem and *learn* what you can do differently to resolve it. Finally, you *take action* to implement your new solutions so that you can deal with the challenge and learn from your experience. The first chapter of this book is spent exploring the Victim Loop, and each following chapter addresses each item of the upper side of the loop: the Accountability Loop.

ACCOUNTABILITY: Taking action that's consistent with our desired outcomes

Knowing your desired outcomes is the key to accountability. If you don't know where you are going, it is impossible to get there:

- For Michael Jordan, it meant going from not making the basketball team in high school to becoming the best player to ever play the game.

- For Steve Jobs, it meant believing he could bring Apple back from the dead to becoming a leader in the computer industry.

- For Oprah Winfrey, it meant rising from a childhood of poverty and abuse to becoming one of the most powerful and influential women in television.

■ For Mahatma Gandhi, it meant pursuing independence for India, against the British Empire. "Gandhi lived, thought, and acted, inspired by the vision of humanity evolving toward a world of peace and harmony," said Martin Luther King, Jr. Gandhi clearly knew where he was going.

Yes, it comes down to walking your talk, but also knowing what talk you are going to walk.

Middle Managers Who Walk Their Talk

I discovered early in my career as a management consultant that the issue of accountability was at the root of most failed change efforts, performance breakdowns, and low employee morale. Since then, our consulting firm has applied accountability systems, practices, and tools to improve organizational, team, and individual performance throughout the world.

Recently, I consulted for a group of twenty middle managers from an international airline company. Right from the start, they complained that senior management was the source of many problems in the organization. The middle managers wouldn't take any responsibility for how they were a contributing factor in the equation. They were stuck in the "victim" mode and completely disempowered. In chapter 1, you will explore the many attitudes and behaviors of being in the victim cycle and how you get disempowered when you travel those waters.

My first goal with this fragmented group was to have them create their own vision of leadership. They needed to see themselves as a unified team and create a picture of success if they were to take charge of improving the organization. In chapter two, you will be guided in a process for taking charge of your success at home or at work so you can improve your life.

Then, I guided them to recognize the breakdowns that caused low profitability and customer dissatisfaction. The list was long. Among them were poor sharing of information, ineffective meetings, and high costs from underutilizing resources. They had to recognize their current reality and address these issues if they were going to actualize their vision. In chapter 3, you will be given a chance to explore your present reality so that you are positioned to effectively address your underlying challenges if you are going to actualize your vision.

Once these problems were identified, the managers saw that they played a role in solving them. Taking ownership rather than passing the buck to senior management was key in regaining their power. In chapter 4, you will explore the impact of taking ownership without blaming yourself or others and how you can reclaim your personal power. Finally, from a place of ownership, they examined their role in the breakdown of the company. They realized that if they came together, they could have a significant influence on the leadership and betterment of the organization. In chapter 6, you will explore powerful methods for self-examination that will lead you to discover root causes and mobilize you to learn to make the necessary changes in your life for getting results.

Six months later, this team had reduced operating costs by 8 percent and increased customer satisfaction by 15 percent. On time departures improved by 20 percent in the same time period.

Pay Attention to What's Important to You

A big piece of the accountability puzzle is paying attention to your current goals. What is on your plate? What do you give your energy to? Where is your focus? What are you accomplishing? It's not just paying attention to your goals, but also your attitudes, thoughts, and actions that will help manifest your dreams. Paying attention keeps your eye on where you are going and helps you make the adjustments to get there.

I often wondered why people resisted accountability. When I started paying attention to my own reasons, I realized it boiled down to three fears: blame, failure, and success. This book takes a look at these fears and how to overcome them.

Fear of Blame

We associate accountability with blame. We fear that if we're accountable for something, we'll be the one to get blamed if it goes wrong. Blame triggers feelings of shame and inadequacy, and nobody wants to feel that. When we avoid being accountable, we might not get blamed for making mistakes, but we end up getting blamed for not accomplishing anything. In chapter 5, we'll explore the antidote to this fear.

Fear of Failure

None of us wants to look bad, make mistakes, or feel incompetent. To avoid feeling that way, we play it small. We stay in what is familiar. We don't challenge ourselves with bigger choices, so we don't have to ever feel inadequate. If we don't take risks, "this" is as good as it gets. The fear of failure prevents us from taking risks that might produce mistakes. But, mistakes are one of the best ways to learn, and learning is the only way to improve. In chapter 7, you will discover ways to transform this fear to your advantage.

Fear of Success

If we increase accountability, we will accomplish more, and we know it. We will gain more responsibility. We will be expected to achieve at a higher level of performance. We will have to maintain excellence. We will have to deal with people's jealousy and our own guilty feelings for outperforming others. That is a lot of pressure. It is strangely easier to dream of success than to actually achieve it. In chapter 8, you will gain methods to overcome this fear.

What Mark Are You Leaving Behind?

When countries miss their economic goals, living conditions decline and people suffer. When a company misses its productivity goals, workers are laid off. When individuals miss their personal goals, they live a life of frustration and anger. Or just not the life they want.

From my talk with Bob that day on the bench, I know I want to look back at my life and enjoy that movie. I want to know that I did the best I could for my family, my career, my community, and my spiritual growth. I want to know that I contributed to peace, that I did my best to make the world a better place, and that I spent time accomplishing what mattered most to me. This doesn't happen by default. It is the result of all the choices we make. I am crafting my life by crafting every moment in it. If I don't, I end up looking back on a life full of missed opportunities, frustrated that I didn't realize my potential, wishing it were different.

You are either going to make an impact on the world by achieving your goals, or your missed goals are going to make an impact on you.

Accountability Takes You to the Moon

What do accountability and NASA's first landing on the moon have in common? Both focus on *recovery*. Just as the trip to the moon was off course 90 percent of the time, the path that takes us to our goal will also get off-course. The first priority is to establish a feedback mechanism to determine whether or not we are on course. The second priority is to develop recovery plans to get back on track as soon as we realize we are not. Then, we launch with our goal in mind. As we get closer and get a better picture of our destination, we keep correcting our course. That was the process that allowed Apollo to reach the moon. Feedback mechanisms based on measurement along with recovery plans keep us on track.

No matter how quickly or radically our environment changes, accountability enables us to adapt to the changing conditions, because the feedback and recovery mechanisms are in place. Thus, we can reach our goals consistently and make a positive impact on our life and everyone connected to it. Align your actions with your goals, pursue them with consistency, and you'll become the most powerful person in your life.

The Rewards of Accountability

Accountability is the backbone of our technology and philosophy of our firm. Recently a client asked me, "Why is all of your work only about accountability?" My answer came as a surprise to me. And it became the impetus for this book. Because accountability is the road to fulfillment. Because it is the only way we can accomplish what matters to us.

The Reward of Trust

Who do we call when we need someone we can trust? Who gets to lead the projects that are most important? Who do we consult when faced with a difficult decision to make? With whom do we choose to share when we want to keep our information confidential? We trust people who have repeatedly done what they said they were going to do. We trust people who keep their agreements. People we can count on. People who are accountable.

And that goes for you and me, as well. When we do the things we said we were going to do, our self-confidence automatically rises. Accountability is a free pass to self-esteem and trust. It gives us the certainty that we will overcome, endure, and keep our word. That we can count on ourselves. That we will get the job done.

The Reward of Achievement

There are rare circumstances in life that bring us more satisfaction than to achieve something that we have set ourselves to achieve. Whether it is running a marathon, spending a whole day without gossiping, or getting out of debt, the moment we know we've done it, we feel alive, we like ourselves a little more, we stand taller, we breathe better. Maybe, for a moment, we are happier.

Accountability is the best-kept secret to happiness. It lets us take command by understanding that success is not accidental, but a proven path of action, learning, and achievement. I believe accountability is the only way we can go from A to Z and create the life we want in between.

The Reward of Recognition

It will be easier to recognize your competence if you participate instead of hiding and playing it small. It might sound simple, but it is true. If you don't put yourself out there, you won't be acknowledged for the great qualities only you know you have. Look back at the people whom you recognize and admire: They demonstrated the best they had. They went at life 100 percent. They were accountable for making things happen. They had a raw talent, and they did what they had to do to optimize it. That is why we have such admiration for professional athletes and exceptional musicians and actors, because we know without a doubt, that they gave their all.

When you give all you have on the job, you become a highly valuable employee. You are recognized as someone who delivers on your promises, and no one wants to lose an employee who can get the job done. The same is true for a spouse, or a friend.

The Reward of Freedom

People have mixed feelings about accountability. Some tend to avoid it because of the myth that it is restrictive, that it means they won't get to do what they want, but what they are told to do. This couldn't be further from the truth. Without accountability, your dreams stay in your bedside journal. Without accountability, you never get to choose what you become.

Without accountability, you are imprisoned by old habits and old beliefs, and you live your life by default.

Accountability gives you *choices*. It gives you the habit of creating new options. It provides the tools you need to transform yourself based on what life you want. You need it to let go of addictions and patterns that prevent you from getting where you want to go. You need it to ask the questions that are going to carry you through. You need it to manifest what you are meant to be.

What's in It for You?

This book is for you if you have ever seen yourself in any of these scenarios:

- If you compare yourself and come short, and that stops you from getting the great job or the new apartment—and you are tired of watching life pass you by.

- If you ever find yourself undermining good opportunities or potential relationships—and you are ready to free yourself from self-sabotage.

- If you hide and act confused when you have made a mistake because the shame you impose on yourself is too great to bear—and you want to replace it with self-support.

- If you ever tell yourself you are not worthy and you keep putting yourself down to prove that you were right—and you have had enough of that.

- If your judgments of yourself and others are so strong that you have a hard time letting anyone get close to you—and you want more intimacy.

- If you are a leader—and you go home worrying about your ability to inspire your people.

- If you are a student—and you find yourself eating one more piece of chocolate or watching one more hour of TV to help you deal with the stress of your exam tomorrow.

- If you are a nurse or taxi driver—and you have nightmares about yet another twelve-hour shift.

- If you are an entrepreneur or in sales—and you are not sure how to make your numbers this month.

- If you are a parent—and you are anxious about not providing your children with the guidance they need to say no to drugs.

- If you are an employee—and you are not sure you will be able to keep up with technology and might lose your job.

- If you are an educator—and you question your ability to convey your passion for learning.

- If you are a flight attendant or business traveler—and flying is not so fun anymore.

The Power of Personal Accountability is for you if you find yourself longing for more freedom—not the kind of freedom where you just do whatever you want in the moment, but a long-term freedom where you are in the driver's seat, and what happens in your life is the result of your *deliberate* intention and action, not a series of random accidents.

Accountability allows you to improve your relationships and clarify your direction. It promotes expansion and growth. It supports risk-taking, and it invites original thinking. It helps you to be someone who inspires others to reinvent themselves, someone who can boost morale and improve customer loyalty. It helps you stay focused and improve your teamwork. It helps you be proactive, instead of crisis oriented. It creates peace and brings people together. It is the next step if you want to expand your ability to love and be loved. It helps you resolve conflicts and increase your self-confidence and trust.

You might want to check out accountability if you could use a little help overcoming adversity. Or if you want to have more fun in life and develop healthy habits. It can increase your mental dominion and help you deal with change, if you want to stop the "blame game" or increase the precision with which you do what you do, if you want to build strong communities and experience optimal health, if you want to know that anything is possible.

Accountability makes this all possible. When you're sitting on that bench, what will you have to say about your life at the end of it?

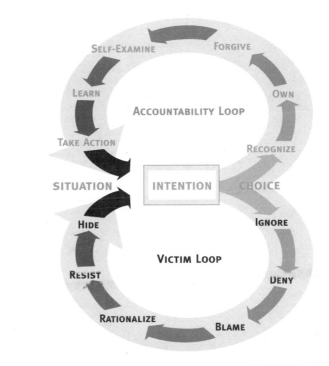

CHAPTER ONE

The Victim Loop *is a way of life where "stuff"
happens to you. You don't seem to have a choice.
Since we all visit it at different times in our lives,
the question to ask yourself is not "How do I not
go there?" but "How fast can I get out of it?" If you
choose the Victim Loop, when faced with a
situation, you ignore, deny, blame, rationalize,
resist, and ultimately hide. As much as we don't
like living there, let's take a look at what happens
when we go to the Victim Loop.*

The Victim Loop

"No snowflake in an avalanche ever feels responsible."
— **VOLTAIRE**

Paula was an intelligent and highly skilled employee. She was hired as an office manager for our consulting firm. My friend Jeff recommended her, and on paper, she seemed to be a perfect fit for the position. Like anyone new on the job, she made mistakes. Oddly, she always had an excuse. She blamed the computers, the employees that worked for her, even clients, and she never apologized or corrected her errors. The morale in her team was plunging, and her leadership qualities were being questioned. She was behaving as a victim, as if she had nothing to do with what was going on.

She rarely took responsibility and never learned from her mistakes. Despite our efforts to assist her in becoming more accountable, her performance never improved, and we finally parted ways.

Jeff stayed in touch with her; she went from job to job showing great promise but never realizing her potential. And she couldn't. She never acknowledged the impact of her attitude and behavior and, therefore, lost the power to do anything about it.

In this chapter, you'll read about the infamous Victim Loop and you'll see how we, ourselves, are often the ones that stop us or sabotage us from getting what we want.

Choosing to Be a Victim

Victim is a paradoxical word. Most people think they are victims when they don't have a choice. When, in fact, it is the opposite: some people *choose* to be victims. You can't always control or change the situation you are in, but you can *always* choose how you respond to the situation, and you certainly have complete control over your *attitude* about it. "Victim? By choice? No way. Not me." That's the response I usually get when I use the word "victim."

Recently, I was driving northbound on La Cienega Boulevard, a major highway leaving the Los Angeles Airport. I was coming back from the East Coast; it had been a bumpy six-hour flight. I was traveling at the forty-five-mile-per-hour speed limit when, out of nowhere, coming from the southbound side of the highway a car hit mine along the entire left side, rendering my car undrivable. He hit and he ran—despite his much-damaged vehicle.

It wasn't my fault. It wasn't fair. Why me? None of these thoughts or responses were helping the situation. I was acting as a victim, and, at the time, I wasn't able to see other choices. As long as I stayed in that state, I was stuck. And resentful. And scared.

When the dust settled and I saw that I wasn't hurt, I started seeing better options. After all, my car protected me well, nobody else was hurt. I could be grateful for that. I had great insurance, and I could be grateful for that. Then I made some quick decisions: Call road assistance, now. Get the escaping vehicle's license plate from one of the incredible number of Good Samaritans who stopped to offer their help. Call my insurance company. Get my office to arrange for a rental car. Find a good body shop in the area. Decide if I needed to get some X-rays. Call my family to reassure them, in case this accident got reported on a local news channel. I was able to move into *action*. The second I got off my victim horse, I was able to take charge and do what needed to be done, efficiently.

One of my goals in life is to be responsive and effective as I maintain a positive attitude. Staying stuck in a victim mentality, I was going to miss that goal.

How often have you found yourself in a similar situation?

Every time you allow yourself to think you have no other choice, you become a victim.

Accountability Is an Option

Life is going to come at you with difficult or even terrible circumstances sometimes. It is its nature. The question is: how will you make the best of it? Some may be born into poverty, contract a disease, or be downsized out of a job. But these events aren't what make you a victim. What makes you a victim is how you *respond* to these events. When you respond with *accountability*, you go on anyway, move forward, and achieve your goals in spite of your difficult circumstances. But when you respond *as a victim*, you begin a downward spiral that moves you further and further away from your goals.

Where does the Victim Loop start and how does it start? It always starts at the same place: you are faced with a situation that requires action on your part and you ignore that you have anything to do with it. That's all it takes.

Victim Responses to a Tough Situation:
The Six Stages

None of us is immune to visiting the Victim Loop. Falling into the victim mode doesn't make you a bad person. There's no need to punish yourself; you are simply being human. It's just a bad choice on the menu of life. But what can you do about it? You can either eat the meal in front of you, despite the fact that it doesn't taste good, or you can order something else.

The sooner you realize you are in the victim mode, the sooner you can recover from it and get back to the business of achieving your goals. But how can you recognize when you are about to enter the Victim Loop?

How can you catch yourself in advance so you don't make the same victim choice over and over again?

Victimhood can sneak up on little cat feet or it can arrive with much fanfare. The best way to catch it—whether it is sneaky or boisterous—is to be aware of its tricks. Here are just a few typical responses to watch out for—in ourselves as well as in others.

#1: Ignore It: "Problem, What Problem?"

This entry into victim mode is a classic. It's called "ignoring" the situation and at some time or another, we all do it. At the office, you may disregard conflicts with your coworkers just to get through the day. At home, you may put off dealing with your aging parents, or perhaps you don't schedule a needed doctor's appointment because you don't want to find out about a potential health issue.

One of the first questions to ask yourself is *why* you are ignoring a problem. You may be ignoring it deliberately, because there may be something more important to deal with at the moment. In this case, you are making a responsible choice.

We live in hectic, complicated times, and not every problem can be solved the moment it appears on our radar screen. We prioritize, and that's a good thing.

But, if what you're really doing is pretending the problem doesn't exist—and hoping all the while that it will disappear all by itself—you've just dipped your toe into the victim pool. Starting with chapter 3, we'll be exploring other responses that might be more satisfying.

#2: Deny It: "It's Not My Problem"

Welcome to the wading pool. You know you've arrived there when you find yourself denying your involvement in the situation. Not sure what it sounds like when you get there? Here's a sampling to help you identify it:

"Sure, there's a problem, but it's not *my* problem."

"Hey, it's not my job."

"Nobody told me."

The reason some people deny they've had anything to do with the problem is because the pressure's building, and they're not willing to take responsibility for it yet. So denial actually makes a lot of sense. But beware; when you start denying ownership of a situation, you also deny yourself the power to do something about it. You've just taken a long step into the pool of victimhood. Now you're actively involved in the situation, but in a negative way and so you have become a part of the problem.

Got your suit on? You are going for a swim.

In chapter 4, you'll discover alternate responses that could get you much closer to a successful outcome.

#3: Blame Someone: "It's Their Fault"

Attention, all victims, prepare to point. That's right, the blaming is about to begin because if I'm not responsible, someone else surely is. And better them than me.

The rules of finger pointing are easy to follow: find someone else to blame, and blame away. At work you can do it with your managers, departments, or associates. At home, kids can blame their parents, and parents, their kids. If you're unhappy with your financial state, you can blame the economy, spiraling unemployment, or budget deficits. But be careful: the blame-game is a double-edged sword, and you will probably get blamed in return. This can go on with no end in sight and only leads us deeper into the Victim Loop.

Are you a strong swimmer? The water's getting deeper.

Unless you enjoy those deep waters, there are other ways to respond, and we'll spend chapter 5 discovering what those are.

#4: Rationalize It: "I Have Evidence"

We now need to prove that this is not our problem. So we look for evidence. Evidence that we don't need to do anything about it. Evidence that someone else is responsible for it. At this stage, meetings get scheduled; surveys are taken; we call friends to support our side of the story. We are trying to justify our lack of ownership. We are trying to demonstrate that our boss's decision was wrong. Or our parents were unfair, and darn it, we are going to prove it. This is the favorite playing field for the mentally gifted. The smarter you are, the easier it is to get trapped in this stage.

At this point, you might be working a lot harder to avoid the situation than would be needed to deal with it. You're now swimming full force, against the current. Chapter 6 will be a good one for you to read a couple of times, if this is your issue.

#5: Resist It: "You're Not My Boss!"

When all else fails—get upset. Why not? It's normal to resist the injustice and tap into the two-year-old inside of us who's struggling to gain control.

You know you're in it when you hear yourself deliver self-righteous pronouncements like:

"It's the principle of the thing."

"I don't work for you."

"You can't make me."

This is the point in the Victim Loop when conflict and irrational action starts escalating. You are far from the original situation, and you are still not dealing with it. In marriages, this is when a debate about who'll take out the garbage turns into a full-on relationship-threatening battle. In work situations, this is when an argument over who is selected to be or not be on a special task force causes people to start sabotaging their careers.

Now you're in the deep end where proving a point is more important than changing your position. You are now wildly flailing in the water.

In chapter 7, you'll read about other alternatives that might get better results than resisting and getting upset.

#6: Hide from It: "Peek-A-Boo, Where Am I?"

This is the last stage of the Victim Loop. Having exhausted all other methods of avoiding the situation, you go into hiding. And as you will see, there are lots of good ways to hide. Here are a few:

Create busy work. Go ahead, overwhelm yourself with meaningless activities. Create unnecessary meetings, paperwork, and projects. Generate a crisis. Feed the rumor mill, share information that doesn't quite exist, withhold information that someone needs. At home, do laundry again, vacuum the carpet, open mail, tattletale on your sibling, do anything to create a diversion and avoid dealing with the real issue at hand. Being confused might be the most effective way of hiding. Agree that the situation must be dealt with, but add that you just don't know how. What's so powerful about this one is that when you stay confused, you can act like you care, when you don't.

Successfully going into hiding means you've effectively completed the Victim Loop. A dubious achievement. But if sitting on the bottom of the pool and drowning in your refusal to act with accountability is where you want to be, congratulations—you've made it. If you are looking for a fulfilling and deliberate life, where what happens is the result of your destiny and your own creating, read on. Chapter 8 might offer some interesting suggestions.

Victimhood Is a Downward Spiral

Here's the strangest thing about the Victim Loop—at some point it takes more effort to play the victim than to be accountable. It's a lot of work to create new ways to blame people, resist being accountable, and find good hiding places.

The ultimate irony is that if you would have been accountable to begin with, you would have successfully dealt with the challenge long ago.

Like a weight-lifter who stops lifting, the muscles atrophy, so it is with accountability. The longer you avoid dealing with challenges, the harder it is to deal with them when they confront us.

In the long run, it's actually *easier* to be accountable.

One of my assignments involved teaching strategic coaching at a high-tech company, which taught strategies for accountable performance management. Two years after taking this class, Tom, a first-level manager, called me for advice. Sue, one of his employees, was spreading rumors about his poor leadership. I asked him what he had done already to resolve the situation. He responded, "At first, I didn't do anything hoping that Sue would stop fabricating these negative stories. When the rumors continued, I asked Sue to stop, but nothing changed. I trusted that the team members were mature enough not to believe her stories."

"Then what happened?" I asked.

He responded a little more sheepishly, "The whole team turned against me."

I asked Tom if he went to the human resources department. He said, "No. I didn't want anyone to think I was a bad manager and couldn't handle my team. Besides, this isn't my doing. Sue should be the one blamed for this problem."

Finally, I asked Tom how bad the situation was. He said, "I went to lunch and when I came back the entire team was gone!" They were all sitting in the HR office.

My advice was simple. Document the rumors and the escalation of the problem. Then, meet with the HR manager to discuss solutions to the problem. After our talk, I asked Tom if he was clear on what to do next. He paused. I could tell something was wrong. Again, he said, "If I go to the HR manager for assistance, they will think I am an ineffective manager."

Tom was stuck in the victim cycle: ignoring the problem, blaming Sue, resisting support, and hiding from those who could best support him.

THE TOXIC EMOTIONS OF THE VICTIM LOOP

Behaviors produce emotions. When you act as a victim, your behaviors create emotions that have the power to poison your personal and interpersonal relationships. The most toxic of these emotions that I've identified are guilt, resentment, and mistrust. Let's explore them further.

Guilt
Even if you won't admit it out loud, you feel bad about yourself when people can't count on you. It lowers your self-esteem and confidence necessary for accomplishing your desired results. You feel guilty about avoiding responsibilities and betraying someone's trust in you. Guilt is a judgment you have against yourself.

Resentment
When you resist accountability, anger is a way to push away the people holding you accountable. You attack others to protect yourself and justify your position. The bitterness spills over into your relationships and negatively colors your perceptions. Resentment is a judgment you have against others.

Mistrust
When you consistently refuse to deal with situations, people stop trusting you. They just are not sure they can count on you. In their eyes, you are always part of the problem and never part of the solution. Mistrust is a judgment others have against you.

So, Now What?

Now you can start to work toward achieving your dreams and goals. You can switch to the other side of the loop. The Accountability Loop. When you move from being a victim to being accountable, you regain power over a life that might feel like it is passing you by. Falling *in* the victim pool is never the issue. The issue is how fast and efficiently are you getting *out* of it? On your way to your ideal life, you will meet challenges and obstacles and that is part of the path. The question is how to overcome them when they show up. The question is, do you have the tools you need to build the life you want? The question is, are you willing to change some of the habits that have gotten you in the situations you want to change? So, how do you get out of this victim cycle?

In the next chapters, you will learn practical strategies and tools for living a life of accountability. Following the order of the Accountability Loop, each chapter will provide an in-depth study of each step in the process of being accountable, including the ways to avoid slipping into the victim cycle. You will also be able to begin putting these strategies and tools to immediate use with exercises at the end of each chapter. You can choose to get out of that exhausting swim in the victim pool.

Grab a towel, dry off, and take a breath; it only gets better from here.

Exercise In preparation for turning your life around or moving to your next level of excellence, make a list of all the situations and relationships at home or at the office that you wish were different. This can include cleaning the garage; confronting Jane, the uncooperative coworker, or Paul, your nonsupportive boss; overcoming hurt from Jack or Betty in your previous relationship; changing careers; learning Spanish; or playing the piano.

Be specific. Write down at least ten areas for improvement. Place an asterisk (*) by those items that are the most important to you. Refer back to this list as you receive additional guidance in the following chapters.

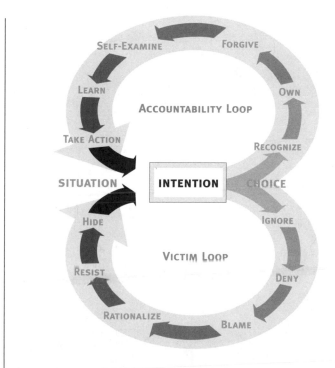

CHAPTER TWO

Taking charge of your life *is no small task. Although it is a simple path, paved with common sense, it certainly is not an easy one to travel. Make it important; stick with it because life is no rehearsal. This is it. Life is happening right now. Make sure you choose your favorite rides.*

two

Take Charge
of Your Life

> "If you want to build a ship, don't gather
> your people and ask them to provide
> wood, prepare tools, assign tasks . . .
> just call them together and raise in their
> minds the longing for the endless sea."
> — **ANTOINE DE SAINT-EXUPERY,**
> **AUTHOR OF *THE LITTLE PRINCE***

Most people don't realize they have choices. They think they are victims of their circumstances, their background. They think, because they were born in this family or with these handicaps, or in that country, they can or cannot do something. There are any number of examples where these truths have been challenged, and people rise up from poverty, people without legs run marathons, and the visually impaired read and write books. Often what is missing is the picture we hold of ourselves. You have to be able to "see" or "think" or "perceive" yourself as a pianist before you can become one. Whether you think you *can* do something or you *cannot*, either way, you are right.

If you don't know what matters to you, it's impossible to achieve it. In this chapter, you will have the opportunity to create a picture of your success. A clear description. Finding a fulfilling job, financial security, the ideal mate, a great college for your kids, that dream house, writing a book that will make a difference, working from home, whatever your thing is—what does it look like? Precisely. Before we can get in touch with this vision of ourselves, we need to clear the deck of limitations.

Perfectionism: The Hidden Show-stopper

We have isolated one of the patterns that is the most paralyzing: *perfectionism*. And it is a dangerous trap. It seduces us, because we think it is required for success. Quite the opposite is true; perfectionism actually *prevents* success. "Perfectionism is the enemy of creation," John Updike said. It *stops* you from taking risks, looking for new perspectives, and solving problems with original thinking. In fear of seeming awkward or being blamed for a mistake, people don't explore creative, alternate ways of thinking. Although excellence is a *process* of continual improvement, perfection is *a final state* against which you judge yourself.

There are many examples of our most successful and innovative leaders who demonstrated imperfection on their way to becoming legends. One such legend was on intimate terms with failure. He failed in business twice and suffered a nervous breakdown. He regularly lost elections including one run at his state legislature, three Congressional bids, two Senate elections, and one bid for the vice presidency. After all those failures, he became our sixteenth president. Abraham Lincoln led the United States through its most crucial period in its history. He won the battle to keep the country united, and he ended the horrific institution of slavery. Lincoln accomplished all of this in spite of his far-from-perfect record of prior losses.

Take Risks Anyway

Part of leading a successful life is taking risks, and you can't wait to be perfect to start taking them. If you think you have to be perfect before you can be successful, you quickly trap yourself in the victim mode because you have just made yourself a victim of your lack of perfection. From there, your slide into the victim mode happens fairly easily as you let your lack of perfection become your excuse for not taking action.

Many years ago I was sitting with Charlie, my mentor. Among his many talents, he wrote extraordinary poetry. He had just recited a poem that brought me to tears and I said, "I wish I could write poetry."

He said, "You can."

"No, I can't," I responded, "I'm not a good writer."

"Hey, no one's grading you." I never forgot.

I realized that this simple statement was holding me back. I was going through life thinking someone was always watching me and "grading" me. My need to write a *perfect* poem was paralyzing me from even making the attempt. Why should I play golf if I won't be a scratch golfer? Why should I submit a proposal to a new client if I don't have the perfect wording on page 5? Why should I ever get married if I can't be a perfect wife? The fear of not being perfect was stopping me from ever taking the risks necessary for having a fulfilling life.

Just look at the Beatles. They were one of the most famous bands, and some people believe they had a near-perfect career. In reality, they are a great example of four people who didn't quit when they had setbacks along the way.

Legend has it that the Fab Four took America by storm and were overnight sensations. This couldn't be further from the truth. The three singles they first released in the U.S. had little or no impact in America. In 1963, Chicago-based Vee Jay Records issued the Beatles' first two U.S. singles: "Please Please Me" and "From Me To You." Neither did well; the latter made it to number 116 on the billboard chart before slipping into obscurity. In September of the same year, "She Loves You" met a similar fate.

It wasn't until December 1963 when Capital Records launched the largest PR campaign in music history around the single "I Want to Hold Your Hand" that the Beatles began to move into their success. The 1964 Beatles American Tour and an appearance on the *Ed Sullivan Show* sealed it, and Beatlemania was born.

The net result of perfection is paralysis. The good news is that being accountable has nothing to do with being perfect.

Becoming an Achiever

So, if perfection's not the key to success, what is? There are three steps that let you make the shift from victim to achiever: creating a clear intention, defining and refining your picture of success, and taking accountable actions. When put in place, you are close to accomplishing your goals.

Step 1: State Your Intentions and Set Your Goals

There is no accountability without intention.

If I told you I ate a hamburger, fries, and a milkshake for lunch, nothing would be wrong with that. But if I told you that my intention was to lose weight and lower my cholesterol, then you would know I was off track. *Intention* is what inspires the blueprint of your new house, your new life. Intention is the launch pad to success. Before you hammer any nails, you need to know what house you are building; you need to define your intentions.

There is an old tale about two shoe salesmen who were sent to some part of Africa to establish the market for shoes.

One communicates back to the home office: "Situation hopeless. No one wears shoes."

The other one reports: "Unlimited opportunity. No one owns shoes."

Different intentions!

When deciding your intentions, be true to yourself. You can create intentions around any goals you want to accomplish. Your imagination is the only limit. So, what's stopping you from achieving anything you want? Maybe you want to be the best salesperson in the dealership; maybe you want to be a great parent, design a great Web site, eradicate cancer, or save the dolphins. Declaring your intention clearly is the foundation for maintaining a positive focus and breaking free from the Victim Loop.

I heard Jim Carrey years ago tell a story during a television interview with Barbara Walters. Jim Carrey's intention was represented by a check that he made out to himself when he was a struggling actor in the mid-1980s. Far from any real prospect of large-scale success, Carrey wrote himself a check in the amount of $10 million "for acting services rendered." For years, he carried the check in his wallet. Later, Carrey explained that it wasn't the specific amount that was important, but the career achievement it represented. His intention was crystal clear. And in 1995,

Carrey did earn a $10 million paycheck for the sequel to one of his most popular movies, *The Mask*.

Intention is the first step and represents your commitment. You still need to figure out what success means for your own challenges and aspirations.

Having an intention puts you on a path of achievement; having a clear intention makes the path easier to follow.

Exercise	Of the original list you created at the end of chapter 1, select the three most important situations and explore your intention for changing the situation. If the situation is a relationship at the office, do you want to mend the relationship, transfer to another division, or quit the company altogether? With your spouse, do you want to work things out and try couples counseling, or seek divorce? In those three situations, drill deeper than "I wish it were different." Different, but how? The increase of clarity will improve your chances of creating what you want.

Step 2: Picture What Success Looks Like to You

One of my dreams growing up was to play on my high school basketball team. Before I entered high school, I went to most of the games. I would imagine myself making the game winning points. On my first day of school, I wrote a letter to myself describing the thrill of being on the court playing with my teammates. I bought a pair of sneakers that I reserved for the opening game. The letter supported me in achieving my dream. Whenever I got discouraged because my playing was off, I would take out the letter and read it to myself as a reminder of my goal. The Los Angeles Lakers were my favorite team. I had posters of Wilt Chamberlain and Jerry West up on my wall. At night, in the privacy of my room, I would try to emulate the moves I saw in the pictures of those athletes. I got myself in shape and read about the mental game and the optimal emotional state to be in. I didn't let the victim conversation take over: the "but I am not so tall" and the "but I am not enough of an athlete." I heard the voices, but redirected my focus to my picture, the basket, practicing with my teammates, the support of a coach, dribbling all the way home. I set myself up to make it happen, and I didn't really care how long it would take for me to do it. I made it important enough to stay on it. I held on to my picture and it carried me through. I not only played on my high school team, but I shone. I will never forget the game where I made the winning basket with only three seconds left on the clock. It matched my picture completely. I still have the shoes I wore in that game. It's difficult to reach a goal if you don't know what it looks, sounds, and feels like. The clearer the picture, the easier it is to accomplish.

REVERSE ENGINEER YOUR PICTURE OF SUCCESS

What did you want to be when you grew up? A famous actor? A pitcher for the Yankees? A clothing designer? You may have had the raw talent to become just that. But, what most of us didn't develop was a *picture* of success capable of pulling us to the top.

I wanted to be a drummer in a famous rock band. I almost made it. I went as far as playing at the Hollywood Bowl. But my picture of success was unfocused. I couldn't sustain the energy it took to have a career in the music business. If you asked me about my mind-set and emotions, my answers would have been vague.

I could have used a large helping of *reverse engineering.* That is the name industrial companies use to describe the process of starting with a final product and working backwards in order to figure out all the elements needed to create it. In my case, such a process would have led me to see myself producing a CD, writing songs, playing them. How do musicians write great songs and deal with record companies? How do they anticipate music trends and deal with different personalities in the band? How do they create a memorable performance and define their unique sound? How often do they need to rehearse?

The questions continue to break down and eventually come together to form a plan that tells us what we have to do this year, this month, this day, and this moment to achieve our dream.

"I never hit a shot even in practice without having a very sharp, in-focus picture of it in my head."
— JACK NICKLAUS

Exercise	Of your short list of situations you would like to see change, pick one and describe a *clear picture* of what you would like to replace the initial situation. You can write a story, make a collage, talk on a tape, or discuss it with a friend. Be as specific as you can. Describe the scene as if it were already happening.

Step 3: Take Action

Once you have a clear intention and picture of success, you are in position to take action. Which one, though? There are too many, or you can't think of any. If you want to lose weight, is it better to start exercising, or should you change your diet? If you change your diet, should you cut out fats, starches, sugars? What if you choose the wrong action? We can end up confused and paralyzed. How many times have you seen management teams rehash old issues without deciding on an action to take? Or the color to repaint the kitchen is in debate for four years? Or the family vacation place is in limbo until the last minute and fewer choices are available?

First, start moving. There really is only one sure way to fail, and that is not to move at all. Take a step, any step. Even if you take the wrong first one, that allows you to get feedback and attempt a different one.

Second, when you do begin to move, take microscopic steps. Taking small incremental steps gets you started. It is easier to fix a small mistake than it is to fix a big one. Movement creates more movement, and as you progress, you will create the safety to take bigger and bigger steps. (Taking action is covered in more detail in chapter 8.)

Sometimes you need to be accountable to others and sometimes to yourself. The cycles are actually similar. You can plunge into the Victim Loop as easily when you are the one you need to be accountable to.

I suffered for six months from an arthritic condition in my hip. I complained, but did nothing about it. I was worried about getting the right treatment, finding the right doctor, taking time away from work, and dealing with the decision of whether or not I would accept surgery as a solution. I knew if I wanted to live a life without pain, I needed to take action. No one else could do it for me. It was my problem. But up to this point, I was paralyzed in fear of doing the wrong thing.

Finally, my wife asked me, "What is the very next action you could take to get some relief?" I needed to make an appointment with a physician, but I didn't know which one. She said that was *not* the first step, because I didn't have what I needed to actually take that step. The first step was to call my friend Paul who had mentioned a great sports doctor in Los Angeles. That was an easy call to make, an easy first step to take.

I called Paul and then the doctor, and I set up the appointment for a consultation. Two weeks after my first appointment, and seven physical therapy sessions later, I experienced no pain; I was done and have not had any pain since. Notice the suffering I put myself through by not taking the very first action, and the next, and the next.

Third, if you are not the one who needs to take the first action, identify who is and by when. It is not enough to know *what* the next step is; the step has to happen. I can't tell you the number of times I meet with groups that spend hours developing an action plan and then leave out *who* is supposed to take action and *when* that action is supposed to take place. Obviously, nothing happens.

I facilitated a team-building session with a management team from one of the largest businesses in the entertainment industry. It was an information technology department, and everyone on the team had experience managing large-scale computer projects. The team identified areas they needed to improve including information sharing, customer service, and project management. We divided the entire management team into three groups, each taking on one of the areas for improvement. Their assignment was to identify actions to be taken that would improve the topic area they were covering and to report their plan to the rest of the team.

The group that worked on improved information sharing reported its results first. It had done a wonderful job of identifying both technical solutions and behavior changes. Some of the solutions included enhancing the company's Web site, developing a process for communicating different kinds of decisions, and establishing a mechanism for sharing updates on projects. At the conclusion of the group's presentation, everyone gave them a round of applause.

Before they could get back to their seats after the presentation, I asked them, "When will all of these tasks be completed?"

They looked at each other in confusion and said, "We didn't plan that far ahead."

I continued the questioning process, "Who is responsible for completing each of those solutions?"

Their answer was, "We didn't get that far in the planning."

Finally, I asked, "If you didn't get that far in the planning, have you scheduled your next meeting?"

Their response was, "We don't have a plan to meet again." We gave them fifteen minutes to complete the action plan and develop a follow-up plan, which they did and reported back to the group.

If we hadn't taken those extra fifteen minutes, they could have become another one of the many teams I have worked with, teams that brainstorm a long list of solutions only to find that people go back to their daily tasks and do nothing to make the improvement. It doesn't matter how good the solutions are. If no one is accountable for taking action, nothing will be done. Nothing will change.

So, What Are *You* Doing?

Two men were carrying rocks on the side of the road. One was complaining and hating every minute of it. The other one was whistling and clearly having a good day. A third man came along and asked, "What are you doing?"

The complainer answered: "Can't you tell? I am carrying rocks."

The whistler answered: "I am building a cathedral."

We don't have to be victims of our circumstances. We can choose to frame what happens in our lives so we win. If we are going to imagine the outcome of a situation, we might as well be a winner in it.

In your life, what are you doing? Carrying rocks or building cathedrals? If you want a life of building cathedrals, *accountability* is for you, and the model described in this book is your blueprint. In the next chapters, you will see how recognizing the situation, owning your part in it, forgiving yourself and other players when mistakes are made, self-examining, learning, and taking action are the steps along a simple path to follow and a proven antidote to the Victim Loop.

| **Exercise** | Define *one* action (remember, keep it microscopic) in each of your initial situations that would make it move, ever so slightly. If you want to move to another country, maybe buy a book about its cities. If you want to change jobs, you could schedule a lunch with someone who does what you dream of doing. If you want to hire a new assistant, you could make a list of the fifteen qualities you would like that person to have. |

CHAPTER THREE

Recognize your current reality. *Call it what it is. Whatever it is. Until you know what you are dealing with and are willing to just state it sincerely, you can't do anything differently. Sometimes, it looks really big. When you shine the light on it, it turns out it wasn't as big as you feared. So, pull out your flashlight.*

chapter | **three**

Recognize Your Current Reality

"It often happens that I wake up at night and begin to think about a serious problem and decide I must tell the pope about it. Then I wake up completely and remember that I am the pope."
— **POPE JOHN XXIII**

As we just discussed, there is no accountability without *intention*. Once you are clear that you want to go somewhere, the next thing to do is to assess your present status.

Take a road map. To get anywhere, you first need to locate two points: where you are and where you want to go. To achieve your goals, the same logic applies. With honesty and courage, you need to call it what it is.

If your intention is to spend more time with your family, for example, the very first question is "how do you spend your time now?" If your intention is to reorganize your office, change your career, re-engineer the manufacturing process in your plant, or help to end world hunger, the work of recognizing your current reality expands accordingly.

A Neutral Frame of Mind

Very much like in the battery of a car—where the positive and negative polarities depend on each other to generate electrical power—a neutral frame of mind has positive and negative elements but does not carry a bias of good or bad. It just is. The reason most people have a hard time assessing the reality of a situation in their own lives is that they can't remain objective and unbiased. When they look critically at their own lives, that analysis comes with judgments and resentments, guilt and disappointments. But the work of accountability requires a *neutral* mind.

To become accountable, you need to really look at what *is*, not what could have been, should have been, or would have been. With a neutral mind, you don't need to feel threatened by the truth. It is what it is, and there is no need to hide or judge. At this point in your journey, you don't need to find solutions or fix anything. You just need to look at what supports your goals, and what doesn't. It is that simple.

It's simple, but it's not necessarily easy. It requires a dedication and persistence to being neutral. Our minds will wander into negative thoughts about ourselves or others. Our feelings will get stirred into disappointment, resentment, or guilt.

Therefore, it takes vigilance to call "time out" to this familiar process and bring back a neutral mind. Some people create their own "recovery plan" by taking a walk or calling a friend when they spin down. Be careful not to select a method for getting back on track that is self-destructive such as overworking or abusing alcohol or painkillers. My favorite used to be food. I would use it when I was challenged by uncomfortable feelings and self-judgment. It worked to calm the critical voices but only temporarily, and my pants size expanded accordingly.

Jack Welch, the retired legendary CEO of GE and *Fortune* magazine's "Manager of the Century," describes the same mind-set when he talks about "GE's decades-old principle of reality." In Robert Slater's book *Get Better or Get Beaten!*, Welch says: "Let me try to describe what we mean by reality. It may sound simple, but getting any organization or group of people to see the world the way it is and not the way they wish it were or hope it will be is not as easy as it sounds. We have to permeate every mind in the company with an attitude, with an atmosphere that allows people—in fact, encourages people—to see things as they are, to deal with the way it is now, not the way they wish it would be."

To ease the journey of having a neutral frame of mind, we recommend you take a few tools in your backpack:

Tool #1: Compassion

This path is one of understanding. There is no need to blame ourselves. If you had *known* how to do any of this better, you would have *done* it better. Trust that the current reality is a great setup for learning. Living is not an easy occupation. Let alone attempting to lead a life that is deliberate, fun, loving, and full of what matters to you.

I have been working for twelve years with an award-winning medical center in Oregon which is one of the most accountable organizations I have come into contact with. They have demonstrated compassionate accountability over and over.

I remember attending a middle management team meeting where the COO announced that they had not been meeting their budget for the last three months. Instead of pointing fingers and finding blame for those involved in the major increase in costs and the mistake in financial analysis, he turned his attention to taking accountability for the problem. He said, "There is nothing gained by finding fault with any one person here. We are all responsible in some ways for the problem, including me. Now we must turn our attention to two things. What can we do to solve the budget crisis by taking immediate action in each of our departments and what can we do to learn from this by creating better forecasting tools?"

After this meeting, each manager got together with his or her team and came up with a plan to cut costs and increase productivity. They didn't take the typical easy, fair approach of "across the board cuts," which could have had a negative impact on patients and caregivers, but made reductions that would preserve the high standards of care and maintain their organizational values. Some managers took larger cuts for their departments so that patient care areas could be sustained close to current resource levels. The focus was on finding solutions that would be best for the entire organization.

Within three months, the organization was back on track. The morale improved as they worked together to resolve this crisis. They also developed more sophisticated financial systems to track results on a monthly basis. The focus on *finding solutions* and the *compassion* that underlined their actions are what allowed them to win and come out of this situation in better shape than they were in the first place. Over the years, it has been during breakdown and crises that they discovered their true strength.

Tool #2: Openness

This is a path of exploration. Be open to experiencing in ways you never have before. Be an investigator; look at the situation from different perspectives.

A few years ago, I worked with a pharmaceutical company in California. The company wanted to change its culture to become more focused on internal customer service. It improved quality standards, reduced project time frames, and increased productivity.

But there was one department of highly educated scientists that refused to make the transition with the rest of the organization. The scientists were arrogant and nonresponsive. They wouldn't participate in cross-functional task forces created to improve internal processes. Their department was stuck, while the rest of the organization was thriving.

After years of attempting to get the Ph.D.s on board unsuccessfully, I suggested to management a radical approach and asked them to be open about it. Leave the Ph.D.s out. Don't invite them to participate. Invite everybody in their department except them. Instead, invite the silent people, those who had been afraid to speak up when the Ph.D.s were in the room. At first, the client was shocked. What if the Ph.D.s walked out? With guidance, they remained open to the suggestion and decided to try this new strategy.

The Ph.D.s were left out and, for awhile, felt like they beat the system because they didn't have to participate in such "nonsense" meetings. Once the assistants were in the meetings by themselves, they declared their support in favor of the change and created action plans for improvement. Within three weeks, they got the feedback from their internal customers that their department had improved dramatically.

Management went back to the Ph.D.s with the great customer feed-back, and asked them if they wanted to stay in the company or not. One quit. The rest started functioning as a team. It took place five years ago, and that was the last they heard of the Ph.D.'s nonparticipation. Manage-ment had the courage to be open to a completely new way of approaching their situation.

Tool #3: Sincerity

This is a journey of awareness. Search for the truth. Be bold. Don't pre-tend. Don't cover up. Don't exaggerate. Don't censure. Call it what it is.

I have been overweight much of my life. I remember one night a few years ago when I realized I wasn't completely honest with myself about it. I decided to make a list of what I knew to be true about my weight:

- My cholesterol was high.

- My breathing was labored.

- I was tight and uncomfortable in my clothes.

- I felt out of control.

- There was a breakdown in integrity between my being accountable and being fat.

- I didn't like photographs of me.

- I didn't know how to solve the problem.

I called it what it was. Before I could do anything about it, I had to see it, look at my problem face to face. I had to acknowledge a reality I had been denying. I had to be sincere and courageous and spell the problem out in details. This step requires no other action than to just *acknowledge* the current reality with *honesty*. There is nothing to *do* about it. Just *call it what it is.*

The Seven Common Causes of Problems

We have identified seven common causes of problems to look for as you analyze your roadblocks to success.

#1: Mishaps

Mishaps are human errors. Basketball players miss free throws; typists hit the wrong key; children forget their homework. Because we are the initiator of these kinds of problems, we have the greatest impact on eliminating them. Developing skills helps, but even the best of the best have mishaps.

#2: Process Failures

Process failures include missed or over-complicated steps to accomplish a goal. At work, it is typical in production lines where the quality control happens too late in the sequence, resulting in wasted materials. At home, there may be no process in place to balance the family checkbook, or no process to take messages and pass them along. The lack of deliberate process causes multiple breakdowns (which is a separate problem, discussed below). We tend to blame people, when in fact the process was never clearly put in place.

#3: Conflicts

Conflicts result from interpersonal differences. People disagree. They have different values, different ideas, different approaches for accomplishing a goal, and different methods for completing a task. But most people hate conflicts, and they will do anything to avoid them. They don't want to risk losing approval, support, or their reputation if they voice a conflict. Unfortunately, conflicts don't just go away. They turn into mistrust, righteousness, and isolation.

#4: Execution Breakdowns

Execution breakdowns are errors in coordination. Execution is the link between people. How do you effectively execute a plan you have agreed to? At work, there are two different projects that relate to each other, yet no one is coordinating the interface, which results in wasted resources and poor decisions. Although *process* breakdowns are commonly addressed in organizations, *execution* breakdowns are often being ignored.

#5: Health Issues

Health issues are problems that relate to our physical body. They can surface from being in an unhealthy environment such as a closed room where everyone is smoking or an office where there are weak fluorescent lights that cause eye strain when reading. We can be overeating, smoking, or drinking alcohol which weaken our body, or we may have a physical health condition that tires us without us knowing it. You can easily be desensitized to a health issue that becomes a root cause for other problems. For example, a person in charge of proofreading almost lost his job until his manager noticed him squinting. Once he got glasses, his performance improved again.

#6: Malfunctions

Malfunctions are errors with equipment. The machinery you are depending on breaks down. That includes software and hardware. Sometimes, the best-laid plans are interrupted when the lawn mower breaks, the computer freezes, or the car dies.

#7: Obstacles

Obstacles are problems out of your control. They occur when your personal or business environment changes around you. Obstacles are barriers that you do not directly create, but they still affect you. This is the cause you can have the least impact on. You can only have an impact on how you *respond* to the obstacle.

Dare to Reach Out

Those are the seven root causes of problems that you might want to identify to fully understand and, eventually, move away from your current reality and toward your goal. However, before you come to any conclusions, make sure to identify the *linkages* and *patterns* between the causes. You may find some surprises at what you can uncover. If this sounds like a tall order, I can tell you an easy way to cut the job down to size: Ask for assistance!

Second opinions are helpful. Not just for medical problems. They can be used to gain a more complete picture of your current reality. Seeking out the perspective of a qualified person who you respect can be an invaluable source of information. He or she may be able to see the big picture and offer a fresh perspective on it. Also, an outsider can see the pieces of your current reality that you may have missed. Finally, it is much easier for someone *outside* the situation to tell you the truth than it is for someone *directly* involved.

That perspective is the reason many CEOs and business professionals hire coaches and why mentoring has become such a major component in the corporate workplace. It is also the reason why many athletes spend so much time and money on personal coaching.

How the Best Become Better

In Michael Jordan's biography, *Playing for Keeps*, writer David Halberstam relates a coaching story that inspired Jordan to strive harder. Dean Smith, the head coach at Jordan's alma mater (and basketball powerhouse) University of North Carolina, helped Jordan play at the next level.

At the end of Jordan's freshman year, Smith showed him a game tape and pointed out Jordan's less-than-stellar defense play. He explained the importance as well as the *need* to be a complete player. In reiterating the value of defensive skills, Smith said, "Michael, do you realize how good you can really be *defensively*?" This conversation caused Jordan to focus on that aspect of his game and become one of the best defensive players in basketball.

But Jordan's seeking out coaching perspectives didn't end when he finished college and became a professional basketball player. After his first season in the NBA, Jordan took aside Roy Williams, another one of his college coaches, and asked, "What do I need to do to work on my game?"

Considering Jordan had just been named the NBA rookie of the year, Williams was understandably surprised and replied, "What more could you need?"

But Jordan was insistent, telling Williams, "I know you'll be honest with me—what can I do to improve myself?" So Williams suggested that he improve his jump shot. Jordan spent the summer doing exactly that, and, by the way, in the 1998 NBA championship games, Jordan's jump shot turned out to be the final and game-winning shot.

Seek Help from More Than One Person

Some people think that reaching out to someone else for advice is an admission of weakness. It's just the opposite. Michael Jordan didn't hire a coach out of *weakness*; he was coming from a place of remarkable *strength*. He had as many as five coaches at one time, each working on a different aspect of his career. Whether you use professional coaches or friends, family members or teammates, religious counselors or therapists, what matters is an outside look at your situation, an observer's point of view.

There are no rules about how many coaches you can use, so find the best person to help you with *each* aspect of your life's ambitions.

I have a health-minded friend. With him, I explore how to eat for optimal health, how to maintain my workout when I am out of town, how to keep my immune system strong while traveling in airplanes all week long. I have a life coach. With her, I talk about balance between work and play, and my creativity. I also have a teammate who helps me with my organizational skills, who shows me how to get things done faster and easier, so I have more time to play and write books. I talk to a therapist when my emotions are out of balance. Some of them I pay; some I take out to lunch; some I trade coaching time based on our different expertise and strengths. I see some once a week, some once a year. What matters is to stay in the game of exploring what works and what doesn't—with an outside pair of eyes.

Coaches don't have to last forever. They bring an expertise I don't have until I integrate the part I need. And when I've learned what I need, I move on—sometimes to the next coach. It saves me time.

| Exercise | Draw up a list of outside people who believe in you, a list of people who demonstrate success in your eyes. These should be people who tell you the truth without judgments or blame, people you believe understand you. For each situation in your life, identify a person who fits this profile. Ask them what you want to know. Buy them lunch or call them and have your questions ready. |

FINDING THE RIGHT COACH

Knowing when you need a coach is one thing, but finding one is another thing altogether. Here are some tips to help you find a coach that will be effective in guiding you to achieve your goals:

1. **Find someone who believes that you can achieve your goal.** A believer will hold a picture of success, and it will be easier to see yourself in that mirror. Make sure your coach is committed to your success based on his or her belief that you can achieve it.

2. **Look for a coach who has accomplished his or her own goals.** Success does breed success, so find a coach who's familiar with the process of achievement. Such people will know from experience that the path isn't smooth. More important, they will have experience with the bumps in the road that need to be overcome, and they'll be able to help you get over them.

3. **Choose a coach who can tell the truth without blame or judgment.** When a coach's valuable observation turns into a criticism, the process quickly deteriorates into *de*struction rather than *con*struction.

4. **Lastly, select a coach who is flexible.** In general, you want to work with someone who is flexible enough to modify his or her feedback, approach, and advice to meet *your individual needs* instead of simply taking a "cookie-cutter" approach of "one size fits all."

You've Got to Be Doing *Something* Right!

We sometimes have the tendency to focus on what we do that *doesn't* work. We have an inner critic who is tougher than any external judge we will ever meet. We do sixty things great but make one mistake, and we kill ourselves over that one. Taking an honest look at your current reality means assessing what needs to change but also assessing what you are doing or what you have done that has contributed to improving, growing, bettering.

It is important to take the time to recognize your greatness, your uniqueness. Acknowledge your good habits so you can keep doing them. *Celebrate your strength.*

If nothing else, it makes it easier to accept the part of you that you want to change. It balances things out. It gives you the self-esteem you need to roll up your sleeves and go to work. To move forward, you need to see the *whole* picture and be aware of what you have working in your favor.

You have now gone from ignoring your current reality to recognizing where you stand in relation to your goal. You have taken your first step out of the Victim Loop. You are moving on.

Chapter 4 is the next step on the ladder to accomplishing what matters to you. After recognizing what it is, we will explore the power that comes from owning a part, any part, of what happens to free ourselves from victimhood.

Exercise	Create a list of the positive attributes and systems that are already in place in your life that you do *not* want to change. Define why each one works for you. It could include the way you organize yourself, or the way you balance your checkbook, or the way you resolve conflicts with others. It could be the way you make decisions, or the way you always send cards on people's birthdays.

Accountability Loop
- Self-Examine
- Forgive
- Learn
- Own
- Take Action
- Recognize
- Situation — Intention — Choice

Victim Loop
- Hide
- Ignore
- Resist
- Deny
- Rationalize
- Blame

CHAPTER FOUR

The power of owning your part. *Once you recognize **what is,** you can assess **what is yours.** In order to change the reality you live in, it needs to be **your** reality. Since you are the creator of the original situation, you can create a different one. Think of the possibilities.*

chapter four

The Power of Owning Your Part

"Most of us can read the writing on the wall; we just assume it is addressed to someone else."
— **IVERN BALL**

When you own something, you are more likely to take care of it. You are more likely to feel responsible. Take a look at the front yard of the typical rented house as opposed to the owned one: which is usually better cared for? The same is true for goals. An owned goal has a much greater chance of reaching fruition than a goal in which no one has a personal stake. Identifying the current reality, which we covered in the last chapter, was the first step. Accepting some ownership forces a personal commitment, without which your goal stays in a rented house. And that is what we'll be exploring in this chapter.

The Problem with Avoiding Ownership

Ownership is the admission fee that lets you in "the solution club." In order to jump-start the creativity to find the best solution, you have to *care*. The problem has to be yours, at least a little. If you don't want to have anything to do with it, it often sticks to the bottom of your shoe until you pay attention to it.

When I find myself in a situation that I don't want to be in, I want out in the worst way. I want to disappear into that crack in the hardwood floor. I want out of my skin. I hate the feeling. It triggers shame, embarrassment, wanting to blame others, and the desire to make it fair. I want to deflect it like my life depended on it. I don't want to own any of it. Especially if it belongs to (fill in the blank): my wife, my boss, my child, the government, or my parent. No way. I don't want any part of it.

Well, sorry to bring the bad news. Someone else might have initiated the problem, but you are now part of it. You wouldn't be thinking about it right now, if you had nothing to do with it. You have created, promoted, or allowed at least *some* of it. And for the record, if you refuse to own any of it, you are a *victim* of it. You don't have access to the information that would lead to the solution. None. You are stuck not only with the problem, but with the feeling that you cannot do anything about it. As we talked about in chapter 1, not doing anything about a problem doesn't solve the problem, it just makes it worse.

What Is the Alternative to Avoiding Ownership?

Take a piece of the problem. Care. Own some of it, even if it's just a small percentage. But make sure you own enough so you can be involved and be creative in developing a solution. Own enough so you can get out of the victim mode and feel like you have a choice in dealing with the situation.

Years ago, I was involved in a personal growth workshop and was asked to tell a story where I had clearly been a victim. I told the story of my stolen backpack in a Parisian subway. I was minding my own business, and the next thing I knew my cash, ticket, and passport were gone. In the workshop, each person had to tell his or her story without taking any responsibility. "Poor me, it wasn't my fault," I said at first.

Then, we were asked to tell the same story taking full responsibility. It didn't take me long to recall the red flags I had ignored. My friend

Jean Paul had told me about a favorite technique to steal from American tourists' backpack carriers in crowded subways. I recollected another red flag about carrying cash instead of traveler's checks. And I remembered my brother, at the airport before I left home, encouraging me to keep my ticket and passport in the hotel safe.

As a victim, I was stuck. I could feel it in my bones. I was upset, whiny, and uncreative. I was building my case of unfairness. I was paralyzed.

But when I was able to shift and own part of the problem I faced, I moved into *action*. I got a new passport. I arranged for cash to be wired to me, and I bought another ticket. I recaptured some of my power, and I moved on.

Exercise Recall a situation that happened to you. First describe it being a total victim. There was nothing you could do to avoid it. Then, describe it with total responsibility. Then answer these questions:

- How did you feel in each situation?

- In which did you feel more empowered to take action?

- What are the benefits and costs of each scenario?

THE CONSEQUENCES PARADOX

When I say that assigning fault and dwelling on who is to blame for past actions is harmful to the process of creating ownership, I don't mean to say that there should not or will not be consequences for past actions. Accountability does not alleviate consequences.

Consequences (i.e., the results of our actions) are a natural occurrence in a world ruled by the dictates of cause and effect. We can't hide from consequences. In fact, when we try to ignore consequences, they usually grow to ever-larger proportions.

For example, Morton Downey, Jr., a pioneer of confrontational TV talk shows, was a striking example of the inexorable nature of consequences. On *The Morton Downey, Jr. Show*, the opinionated host chain-smoked cigarettes, often blowing smoke in his guests' faces as a sign of displeasure.

Downey was a militant smoker, who consumed a pack of cigarettes or more a day from the age of thirteen and who voraciously argued for smokers' rights. In 1996, the consequences of almost a half century of smoking struck home, and he was diagnosed with lung cancer.

To his credit, Downey treated his cancer as a wake-up call. He became a high-profile *opponent* of the tobacco industry. He filmed public service announcements, and in interviews, he described himself as "an idiot" for smoking. Downey took *responsibility* and *accountability* for his actions, but there was no way to evade their consequences. He lost his battle with cancer at age sixty-seven. Downey did, however, make an important point: We can control *how we react* to consequences. He showed that we can treat them as learning experiences and that we can use them as *opportunities for personal growth*.

Owning 100 Percent of a Project

What I'm about to say is going to have a lot of math teachers rolling their eyes. And I was a math teacher so I know this doesn't add up—at least not in mathematical terms. But in accountability terms, it does. Each person involved in a project owns 100 percent share of the project's success. If ten of us share a project, we each own 100 percent which adds up to 1000 percent, in *accountability* land. We all need to think of ourselves as owners of a project. Whatever the role you play, whatever your position in the field, whatever your level in your organization, what needs to be done, needs to be done.

We *do* need to own the whole project, but at the same time, we need to recognize and respect the roles of everyone involved in the project. When we accomplish that, we temporarily suspend the laws of mathematics and allow everyone to benefit from a *100 percent ownership* stake.

Beware: Ownership Traps

Sometimes, when there are several contributors to a situation, people can get sidetracked by measuring their *share* of ownership. When this happens, measuring ownership can quickly become a roadblock to success. We have identified three traps to watch for: power, martyrdom and denial-blame.

#1: The Power Trap

This trap springs up when someone declares ownership so that he can take control of a project. Jill was the manager of auditing parts at one of the major Japanese automakers I consulted for. The company's auditing systems, which involved controlling inventory, managing budgets and shipping parts to dealers, were in major need of modernizing. Upper management finally supported the funding of a project to add a new technological system to improve the auditing function. A project team was formed to first recommend which new technology would be purchased (a three-month task) and then to plan the installation process (a twelve-month task).

The project team included a group from the auditing department and a group from the information technology department. Here is where the fight began. Both departments wanted to lead the project. Whenever they met, the parties would end up in conflict. After several weeks, the senior manager in charge of the project ordered another technology-related department to get involved and chose that group to lead the project team.

The new technology department tried to conduct meetings, but members of one team or another wouldn't show up, assignments weren't completed, and information wasn't being shared. So, the new project leader decided to manage the project by keeping all parties separate so that they wouldn't fight with each other. The planning stage took five months instead of three, and their recommendation was to spend $1.5 million to do a study to find out which technology to use. Needless to say, senior management was furious about this recommendation.

All three parties were caught in their own version of the power trap. Everyone loses when this game is played, as you can see from this story. Finally, a consultant was brought in to assist the team in facing its issues instead of denying their involvement and blaming others. The consultant facilitated a team session, with all three groups on the project team, and they worked out the trust issues. The team developed a new vision for completing the project, followed by clear action steps to improve performance execution and to track results. They also set up a mechanism to support one another. They were able to get their project back on track according to their revised project schedule.

The long-term effect of this "project ownership" did not help achieve the company's larger goal; instead, it created *anger* and *disengagement*. The project took longer to complete. The overall disharmony within the two divisions of the company took a long time to resolve. In other words, they created a lose-lose situation.

#2: The Martyr Trap

This trap springs up when we take *all the blame* for a situation. The martyr trap occurred while I was working for a nonprofit organization devoted to building decent housing for people around the world who couldn't otherwise afford it and have them participate in the construction of their homes. Carol, one of the organization's managers, was having a problem with Sandy, her administrative assistant. Sandy's work was of good quality, but she was consistently late in completing her assignments. Carol mostly ignored the problem—until it reached a point where it reflected poorly on the entire department and was viewed as a bad internal customer-service issue.

When I talked with Carol about the issue, she responded, "You can't blame Sandy, because the quality of her work is good. Besides, she is virtually a volunteer, working at a salary much less than she could get if she were in a private business." Of course, this response didn't solve the problem.

While consulting with Carol on her leadership approach, we surfaced her guilty feelings about coaching an employee who was such a committed team player and whose work quality was good. I pointed out that a good team player who produces good quality work probably has it within her to be more timely in her response if she were given some training or coaching.

Carol saw that giving feedback to Sandy could be *an opportunity for her to improve*, rather than a *punishment* for being late with her assignments. Carol spoke with Sandy about the problem in a compassionate manner, but she was clear on Sandy's need to improve for the good of the department and the organization as a whole. Carol then arranged for Sandy to meet with a productivity consultant, who focused on getting things done, using an organized planning system.

After the coaching session, Carol had a meeting with Sandy, reviewed what she had learned, and then gave Sandy time to put the new organizational system in place. Sandy was successful, and so was the department in improving customer satisfaction. Sandy felt more committed to her job and the organization, while Carol's status as an effective leader rose to new heights.

The martyr trap can happen when an employee takes all the blame for a colleague's incompetent actions. The "martyr" may be doing it out of support, but is taking the power away from the employee. By prohibiting the person from *owning* the mistake, he or she will most likely not learn anything and will continue to repeat the *same* mistake.

#3: The Denial-Blame Trap

This one springs up whenever someone uses ownership to *sidestep* accountability. Imagine two drivers pulling out of their spots at the parking lot of a shopping mall and reaching the same area at the same time. This accident was caused by the carelessness of *both* drivers. But suddenly one driver jumps out of his car, points his finger at the other driver, and says she is *more* to blame than he is. This is a direct attempt to deny ownership.

In each of these traps, ownership is inappropriate, and there's either too much or not enough. It leaves one or both participants frustrated, angry, or helpless.

What Part Do You Play?

Ownership is a play with three possible characters: the doer, the overseer, and the helper.

1. **Doer:** You are a doer if you are *directly* involved in the situation and the solution. In the work-related example, Sandy was *directly involved in the situation*, because it was *her* performance that needed improving. She was also *directly involved in the solution*, because she had to change her habit of turning in her assignments late.

2. **Overseer:** You are an overseer if you are *indirectly involved in the situation* and *directly involved in the solution*. Carol, the manager overseeing Sandy, was *indirectly involved in the situation*, because she didn't perform any of the functions related to Sandy's assignments. However, Carol was *directly involved in the solution*, because Sandy's performance reflected on the department's reputation, which was Carol's accountability.

3. **Helper:** You are a helper if you are *not involved in the situation*, but you are *indirectly involved in the solution*. Paula, the productivity consultant, educated Sandy on a system that she could use to improve her ability to get her assignments done on time with less stress. Paula was *not involved in the situation*, but she was *indirectly involved in the solution*, because she was the coach who provided Sandy with the tools needed for solving the problem.

Sandy, Carol, and Paula were equally accountable, each 100 percent, as we have already established in our "weird math" table.

The *doer* is the closest to the situation. For example, if my daughter has some homework, she is the doer. She is ultimately responsible for delivering the product. As a parent, I am an *overseer*. If I see that she is cruising, I don't need to be involved, I am just observing, which is not a minor job. By observing, I stay in touch with what needs to happen. As quiet as this role is, it is a critical one.

If my daughter struggles, I become a *helper*. I get involved and assist her as much as I can. I might hire a tutor, who is a helper, if I can't provide the help she needs. I also go back to being an *overseer* to ensure the tutor is effective and my daughter is successful as a result.

In this context, my daughter, the tutor, and I are equally involved in making my daughter successful, even if the doer is the one ultimately delivering.

Ownership increases your *involvement*. It gives you the impetus to do your very best. It opens the flow of *creativity*, and it allows you to access an *intuition* and *energy* that only comes if you care, if you are involved. You are getting out of the victim loop and using *accountability* to own more of the outcome than you knew was yours to own.

Get ready to reap the rewards. As you have now recognized and owned part of the problem, you are about to discover, in the next chapter, the best-kept secret in the voyage of finding freedom: self-forgiveness.

HOW ONE WOMAN TURNED A PERSONAL LOSS INTO A PUBLIC CRUSADE

Ordinary people can accomplish extraordinary things when they make a situation their own. Candy Lightner's response to the tragic death of her thirteen-year-old daughter, Cari, is a poignant example. In 1980, a drunken driver, who had been released on bail after a hit-and-run accident just two days before, killed Cari. The driver had multiple DUI accidents and convictions on his record, and yet he was still allowed to keep his license.

The grief and anger that Lightner experienced in response to her daughter's death was not unusual, but the way she chose to deal with her loss was. "I promised myself on the day of Cari's death that I would fight to make this needless homicide count for something in the years ahead," she wrote in her book, *Giving Sorrow Words*.

A few days after her daughter's funeral, Lightner met with a group of friends, and the idea for MADD, Mothers Against Drunk Driving, was born. Lightner had taken ownership of an ambitious project—she planned to prevent the tens of thousands of deaths caused by drunk driving each year. In the two decades since, MADD has been instrumental in reducing alcohol-related traffic deaths by 38 percent, and *more than 138,000 lives have been saved*. On its twentieth anniversary, MADD had three million members and more than six hundred local chapters throughout North America.

It is worth asking what might have happened if Candy Lightner had not taken a solution-oriented approach to Cari's death and, instead, had become mired in the situation itself. She could have succumbed to the grief and depression that naturally follows the death of a loved one. Or, she might have devoted her energy to ensuring the driver was punished and never founded MADD.

For more information about MADD, go to www.MADD.org.

Exercise	Make a list of situations where you have felt victimized, where you felt you had nothing to do with a problem that arose. Something just "happened" to you. Then re-look at each situation, and find ways to take more ownership for your part of the problem. You might identify where you were a doer, an overseer, or a helper.

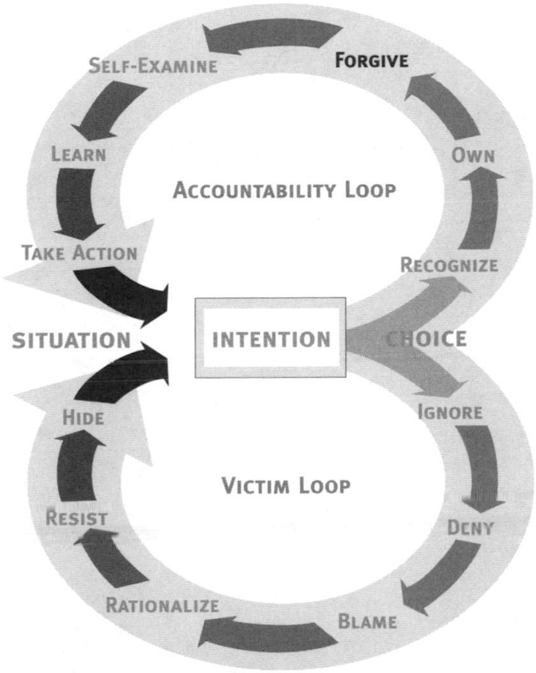
SELF-EXAMINE
FORGIVE
LEARN
OWN
ACCOUNTABILITY LOOP
TAKE ACTION
RECOGNIZE
SITUATION
INTENTION
CHOICE
HIDE
IGNORE
VICTIM LOOP
RESIST
DENY
RATIONALIZE
BLAME

CHAPTER FIVE

The gift of forgiveness. *Once you have recognized the reality of what you are dealing with and owned the part you have played to get there, forgiveness is your way out. Not an excuse to do something that didn't work again but an opportunity to wipe the slate clean and give it another shot.*

The Gift of Forgiveness

"The old law of 'an eye for an eye'
leaves everybody blind."
— MARTIN LUTHER KING, JR.

Once you have identified a situation and owned your part, you've opened up the can of criticism. This is the step where people tend to run away. After all, who wants to willingly be put on the line and be attacked by others or, worse, by themselves? No matter how big or small, external or internal, the attacking criticism is hard to bear. It would be simpler to go back to the old way of finding excuses or blaming others. In this chapter, we will take a fresh look at an ancient technique. Whether directed at others or ourselves, forgiveness is the way out of this self-defeating cycle.

Mistakes Come with the Territory

I believe in the good nature of people. I believe people strive to do the right thing. Sometimes, they miss the mark. But who cares? To make a difference, to pioneer and invent, to break old paradigms, you have to experiment, try new ways. In doing that, you may fumble and stumble and look awkward, but I ask again, who cares? Who is watching? Who is grading? Maybe you're thinking your boss is, or your spouse. But hey, if you are doing your best, there is nothing more you can do. Ideally, we wouldn't judge ourselves or others. But if you do, forgiveness is your return ticket. It brings you back to health, happiness, and caring.

> "I'm never looking back and seeing how bad I played. I'm looking forward to tomorrow to see how good I can play."
> — **MICHAEL JORDAN**

Letting Go: A Zen Tale

A young monk was traveling with an older monk when they came to a river. On the bank was an attractive, finely clothed young woman who could not cross the river without ruining her gown. The young monk heeded his vows to avoid contact with the opposite sex, and he looked away. But his elder walked directly to the woman and offered his help. He carried her across the muddy river and put her down. After thanking him, the woman and the monks parted ways.

The young monk was shocked by the elder's behavior, and he silently stewed about it, until hours later he could not hold his tongue any longer. "How could you do that?" he complained. "It is a violation to even look at a woman and you spoke with her. You carried her!"

The older monk thought about his young companion's criticism and smiling, he replied, "I put her down on the other side of the river hours ago, but you are still carrying her."

Self-Denigrating Thoughts—Be Gone

To get on with the process of life, we have to let go of those stewing conversations we do internally or around the coffee machine with our co-workers or our best friend. The "*I can't believe I just said that*" and "*I wish I could be more like him.*" All the versions of "*She probably doesn't like me*" and "*I am too fat.*" From the "*I don't deserve this*" to "*This is unfair,*" "*A good manager wouldn't do that,*" "*I am never going to make it,*" "*An employee should be more dedicated.*" And one of my personal favorites, "*I am not good enough.*"

You can choose to get out of this internal hell. I heard a story, years ago, about a Tibetan monk who was interviewed by a journalist. The Tibetan monk said, "It's like I have two dogs fighting inside of me; one represents negativity, and the other beauty and positive thoughts."

The interviewer then asked, "Well, which one wins?"

The monk replied, "Whichever I feed the most."

Forgiveness Is the "Opt-Out" Button

Forgiving others—and one's self—is like hitting the "un-subscribe" button in response to those annoying e-mails you get, which you never asked for. That unsolicited spam is just there, taking up space in your e-mail in-box, taking time in your day. They don't add anything; they're just a nuisance. The same is true of those judgments: they take the place of creative thoughts, of loving thoughts.

Of all the things you are accountable for, what you allow to float in your head is probably the most important one. It is more internal, quieter. But it impacts your inner experience. It impacts how you feel about yourself. It impacts the way you drive, the way you perform at the office. If you tell yourself you are not good enough, well, you won't be. I want to *choose* what is on my hard drive. I don't want my brain to be polluted. I want to think of people I love or stories I want to tell my kids tonight. I want to have *supportive* thoughts. I want to brainstorm ideas for a new book, or think of vacations I want to take, or dream of a new job or a new car, or meditate quietly. I want to remember my walk this morning, or pray, or think whatever I want, *deliberately*, not by default. And I can't receive this gift of freedom if I am busy stewing, judging, complaining, or wishing my life was different.

A Process of Understanding and Moving on

This morning, Mary was late for an important meeting. I got the pinching sensation I feel in my stomach when I formulate a judgment. I realized immediately that her lateness was going to annoy me throughout the meeting and maybe longer. I breathed deeply a couple of times and walked myself through a deliberate path of thoughts. I am late sometimes, so I should check with her, to make sure everything is all right. After all, it doesn't happen often with her. I also want to tell her that I need her to commit to do her best to get here early, to be sure to be on time. I wrote a note to myself to talk to her about it, and I moved on with my meeting.

Forgiveness is a vacuum cleaner. It can clean cobwebs and dust piles. Use it without moderation. Use it every day. Every time you experience your version of "the pinch." It is simple—not easy, but simple. The more you use it, the easier it gets.

My friend David Allen, author of *Gettings Things Done*, has a technique he uses and teaches. Every time he experiences a tension, he writes an affirmation. If his waiter is really slow in a restaurant, he writes "I am grateful to have a little time to myself." If an associate misses a deadline, he writes, "I am glad to work with people I can talk to honestly and feel safe" before he goes and addresses the lateness with this person. If someone cuts him off on the freeway, he even has a little tape recorder so he can speak his affirmation instead of writing it and be safe while he drives. "I enjoy my car, and I am glad I am not in a hurry."

Not a Substitute for Corrective Action

Forgiveness allows you to come to the action in a more creative, caring way. I walked into my office the other day to find Beth, our accountant, frantically looking for a check she remembered printing but not sending. She just couldn't find it. I could see she was mentally bashing herself over it. I mentioned looking in the book she puts the checks in so they can easily be signed, and asked if she had searched there. She brushed off my suggestion and kept going with her self-judgment and frantic energy.

Seeing I couldn't do much for her, I thanked her for being so caring and told her I trusted the check couldn't have disappeared, and I was sure she would find it. I also suggested she call the few other vendors she had mailed checks to and verify that they didn't receive two. And I moved on with my day. A few hours later she came into my office triumphant. She had found it. It was in the book she puts the checks in to be signed. I smiled and suggested that her own self-judgments made her deaf and unable to hear the solution.

A few years ago, I was coaching Gary, one my associates, who had to make an eight-hour presentation on strategic coaching, a topic he hadn't presented before. It was a grueling three hours of coaching and course correction. After forty-five minutes, he asked me for a break so that he could do a process we learned at the University of Santa Monica. This process was called "self-forgiveness." Using this process, we would move into the most *compassionate* place we could muster at the time and recite the following phrase for each of our topics of self-judgment. "I forgive myself for judging myself as _____." Gary said, "I forgive myself for judging myself as a person who doesn't learn fast enough." He also applied the technique to many other self-criticisms. "I forgive myself for not being a good enough consultant, not having enough experience, and not being dynamic enough."

When he came back, he said, "Okay, I'm ready for more corrective feedback." The technique had worked. Gary was calm, open, and ready to hear more feedback on the next section of the training program. He added, "I was starting to get down on myself, and I couldn't focus on learning from your feedback. Now I feel better and am ready to continue."

Although I knew this technique was powerful for neutralizing self-judgment, I never thought of using it in the middle of the process, while the judgment was being formulated. The faster, the better. He took three more breaks to do more self-forgiveness before we were finished. The next week, he gave a fantastic presentation for a group of highly trained managers. The participants evaluated his presentation with excellent scores, and his presentation led to five additional training programs. Gary clearly demonstrated the power of self-forgiveness.

80 Percent Eyes in Front of You, 20 Percent Rear-View Mirror

As bold as it sounds, you choose what you think of, what trots in your head. A good rule of thumb is that if a thought *serves* you, it is welcome to stay. But if it *paralyzes* you—e.g., if it prevents you from writing a book, singing at the top of your lungs, or advancing your career—it has to go. Period. If that memory causes you to drink, overeat, smoke, veg out in front of the tube, or be angry at your kids, it can't stay. If it isn't supportive, it's *out*. It's that simple.

My friend Karen was in between jobs. She had managed a jewelry store, but hadn't like the job much. In fact, she was clear that she only worked for the money. Her real passion was design. She wished she could be an interior decorator. At lunch, I confronted her. I asked her, since she was in between jobs, why not gear toward her passion for her next job?

I listened to the laundry list of all the reasons why she couldn't, shouldn't, wouldn't. She wasn't good enough. She had tried working on her own in the past and had failed. She had lost money. She struggled and didn't get anywhere. I asked her when that other attempt took place. When she was twenty-one. She was now forty-four.

Well, needless to say, we embarked on a long discussion addressing each and every one of her beliefs that she was holding on to. We looked at all her judgments and deconstructed them. None of them were supporting her in doing what she really wanted. We applied my friend David's affirmation technique. "I am talented and it is fun to take risks" was one of the affirmations she decided to copy on Post-its and put around her house. She realized "I am not good enough" was also an affirmation—except, that one, was pulling her away from her dream.

After our conversation, Karen agreed to take a step toward her life's passion. She started talking with a life coach, and a few months later was working as the assistant of one of the greatest decorators in Paris. She's planning to start her own practice in the next year.

Forgiveness Is a Deliberate Act

Ignoring just won't cut it. If you have judgments, denying that you think what you think and feel what you feel is just not going to work. If not dealt with, those feelings will spill into other areas. Without knowing why, you'll want to kill the driver next to you in traffic. You might think it is not related, but you will be unable to get on an elevator or sleep at night. You'll sabotage a potential courtship. You'll freeze when it is your turn to talk at a meeting. You will be heavily in debt or chronically sick.

It's not worth it. Acknowledge what is. My friend Sam recently went through this. He had been the director of a pharmaceutical company for about ten years when he came over for dinner. Between salad and dessert, he announced that he had just gotten fired. He started crying. After expressing my compassion, I started asking questions. As described in the previous chapters, I assisted Sam in seeing the situation for what it was, with honesty. He told me he had been unhappy for quite some time. He was leaving the office earlier every day. The job wasn't so interesting to him anymore, and he actually didn't enjoy working with the people he worked with.

I invited him to take *ownership* in the situation and see the part he had played in the decline of their collaboration. Sincerely, he started sharing that he had lost interest in the company about two years ago. He said he was going through the motions but his heart wasn't in it. He really didn't like the way the company was managed by the upper level. He was resentful, but he had never really said anything about it.

I asked if he was interested in doing some "self forgiveness." He had always teased me a little about my technique, but he was in so much pain that he was willing to try. I got him some blank paper, I lit a candle, and I put on some soft music. He wrote, "I forgive myself for judging myself for" and started filling in the blanks: "I forgive myself for judging myself for losing interest in my job," "I forgive myself for judging myself for not communicating with the other executives," "I forgive myself for judging myself for feeling bruised that they fired me first." He went on for an hour.

I gave him all the space he needed, and when he came out of that room, he looked wasted and sad; still, there was something different in his eyes. He said he felt less upset. He had a sense of where to go from here. A few months later, he started his own coaching practice. Now he is blossoming.

Hurt People Hurt People

They hurt themselves, and they hurt others. Sometime in your life, last week or growing up, you have felt pain. If you have families, friends, pets, or partners, you have felt pain. You may have been betrayed, or you had to deal with death, frustration, or humiliation. As a reaction, you may start fearing, attacking, judging, and developing ways that would protect you from feeling that way again. You may establish mechanisms to protect against difficult feelings, to the point of not feeling anything anymore. You may conform to what is expected of you so you won't be rejected. You may drink, smoke, over-eat, or swallow pills to numb this unbearable pain. You may put some distance between you and those who caused the pain—and from the ones who look like them. You have a responsibility to what you were given. If you keep it and start acting out because of it, it is yours. It is your responsibility to question and heal so you won't carry the pain over. A measure I use for myself to stay away from "right and wrong" is to ask myself: "Does this work or does it not?" If not, I put something else in place. Sometimes it takes time; sometimes it is instant. Whatever it is, if it doesn't work, based on your own opinion, move in the direction of something else.

My friend Christine experienced this. She had been hit by her father when she was young. He was an alcoholic, and she could never know how he was going to respond at any given moment. I met her in a self-help workshop. We had lunch and she told me she had recently come out of a three-year relationship with the father of her two-year-old daughter. He was a social drinker, until he lost his job and started drinking more. She came home one night; he was alone with their daughter, who was one year old at the time. He was drunk and started acting belligerently. She just felt it again: the same gut-wrenching feeling she used to have when she would come home from school to an extremely happy father or an angry father, or a sleeping father—and a sad and depressed mother.

She woke up. She saw that she had to do some work to get out of this familiar pattern. She had to heal so her daughter and she wouldn't have to live with constant knots in their stomachs. That night, she packed and got herself into an Al-anon meeting, the twelve-step program designed for the significant other of an addict. When I met Christine, she was in recovery, reconstructing her life and her daughter's. She passed on a heritage that didn't work for her and had the courage to break the cycle so her daughter wouldn't get hurt like she did.

Stuffing the pain doesn't work. Your unconscious becomes like a closet full of sadness never expressed, fear never calmed down, swallowed anger, secrets non-disclosed, explanations you've never asked for. The work of accountability is to empty this closet and make sure what you keep is deliberately chosen, and not piles of old stuff you don't even remember putting there in the first place. To build a solid house, you must make sure the basement is free of any termites.

Forgiveness Is Universal

To practice the forgiveness we talk about in this book, you can be a member of any religion, any faith, any spiritual practice, or you can have no faith in anything. You don't need to go to a specific place of worship, and there's no need for prayer or sacred assemblies. This forgiveness gets practiced *by* you, *for* you. It is practical, daily, pragmatic. You can do it alone, accompanied by a coach, or in front of a fireplace with a group of friends. You can be at home or in nature. It can take two minutes or two years. It can be a painful journey or a joyful celebration. However you want to do it, it is your choice. What matters is to do it. Just that.

Forgiveness is an antibiotic. As discussed in earlier chapters, it cancels the effect of a bacteria called self-criticism, judgment, resentment, guilt, and all those colorful feelings that decay our lives. There are no contra-indications and no side effects. It is the antidote without which you don't live a full life.

Forgiving is not agreeing, validating, or excusing. It is not biting your tongue in resentment, while cursing the other person under your breath. It is not a favor you give to the one who hurt you, allowing him or her to do it again. Forgiveness is sometimes a difficult pill to swallow because it often means having to take some responsibility, reopening your heart, and risking getting hurt again, to accept your limits and those of your loved ones.

The purpose of forgiveness is to let go of the baggage you don't need. The question here is not to address if you were right or wrong, if the other person should be punished or not, or if he or she deserves to be forgiven. Each person has his or her unique value system, and it would be impossible to address all of them here. What matters is that forgiveness is done for your own benefit. In simple terms, you are happier when you are able to forgive. You become free because your actions are deliberate and not the mere results of uncontrollable impulse—and also because forgiveness is a higher road.

Six Steps to Forgiveness

Forgiveness doesn't just happen. Healing doesn't just happen. It is a process you need to go through. We have identified five stages that seem to occur on the way to freedom, which is the sixth and final stage. This doesn't mean you necessarily go through all of them. You can also go through the whole cycle in a short amount of time. This is just a guide to support you in moving from one stage to the other by following simple steps. At each stage, I've offered an example to illustrate how each step can affect the people involved.

Step 1: "I am upset at (my parents, my boss, myself, God . . .)"

Whether you have been wronged, abused, abandoned, fired, rejected, or criticized, your buttons have been pushed. You may not express it externally, but you are mad about something. *Allowing* those difficult feelings to surface, and realizing they exist, is a necessary step. Repressing keeps you stuck. Spilling them all over the place fuels the fire uncontrollably. And that doesn't work either.

To see how this can play out in a personal relationship, consider the experience of my friend Diane, who was married to Paul for six years. She could never do anything right. If she cooked fish, he wanted meat. If she stayed home, he was annoyed; if she worked, he was frustrated. When Diane started therapy, she became aware of how critical he was. She got upset realizing all the instances she had felt badly about herself under his critical microscope.

In this phase, I recommend finding a constructive environment to express feelings without hurting anyone, including you. You might go for a run, paint a canvas, or talk to a friend who is not involved in the drama. You could meditate, pray, or go visit an old aunt in her hospice. This phase doesn't include getting drunk, driving like a maniac, barking at the parking attendant or at your kid for spilling the milk at dinner, or any other diverted reaction.

Step 2: "I am hurt because . . ."

Once the upset is uncovered, we often get in touch with a deeper feeling of hurt. You would not be upset if you didn't care. Diane stayed in that phase for a while after she saw the reality of her relationship with Paul. She was inconsolable. She had put so much into the relationship. She was disappointed that she had wasted time with him. She would play all these movies in her head of all the times she had let herself down. She also felt for him; she knew his father and he was very critical. And she loved Paul. And that upset her even more. If only he could pull himself together and stop the criticism, they could be so happy.

Here, too, it is important to let those feelings out. You might watch a sad movie, write a letter, look through old pictures, go to your place of faith, or talk to a therapist. Sometimes, my daughter and I read a book about Helen Keller that makes us sob. Just to make ourselves cry and be moved. *Not* dealing with feelings might translate into overeating, being distracted at your job, spending impulsively, or getting sick or depressed.

Step 3: "I am concerned (worried, afraid . . .)"

Once you get in touch with your hurt, you often move to fear and worry. Diane was afraid of being alone. She didn't want to stay in her destructive relationship with Paul, but she was also mortified at the idea of starting on her own: getting back into the dating game, dealing with the divorce itself. If Paul had been so critical while they were together, she wondered, what was he going to be like in the thrust of a separation? She was worried she could never get out of this dynamic and would attract another critical person. And, she worried about not pulling it off financially on her own.

The way out of this phase is to breathe, relax, and trust that there is an end to this tunnel. Recognize that you are going to have the strength to handle the situation confronting you, that you're going to be okay. Do whatever you do to relax yourself: hug your child, pray, read something that inspires you, go to a museum, ask someone you love to tell you what is great about you. Do anything to carry you through: you are almost there!

Step 4: "It IS my fault"

This phase stinks. But it is your ticket out of here. When you can take some responsibility, you are home free. Until you do that, you are stuck. The idea here is to transition from *blaming* yourself and feeling like you have done something *wrong* to *taking ownership* for your part of it. As soon as you can do that, you take dominion over it, and you are no longer under its spell.

Diane had a memorable moment one evening when I was with her. She reminded me of Audrey Hepburn running around singing, "the rain in Spain stays mainly in the plain." Diane kept saying, "I did it, I did it," running around the room. Past the emotional outburst, I asked her what she really meant. She said she saw the payoff she was getting from staying in an abusive relationship: It had allowed her to avoid intimacy, which she knew she feared. His abuse kept her at a distance, and that served her well.

It is not unusual for people to have a spiritual awakening in this phase, to uncover deep feelings of compassion, or to reveal unconditional love.

Here, we suggest that you did your very best and the other players did their best as well. Let go of the guilt—and the resentment. It is unproductive, unkind, and overall unnecessary. I started a ritual ten years ago, when I didn't get a job I really wanted for what I thought was the most interesting PR firm in France. All the partners came from the theater, and every event they put on had an artistic slant to it. The partners once planted wheat on crates in farms around Paris and brought them on trucks to the Champs Elysees. When Parisians woke up, the most beautiful avenue in the world was covered with a wheat field. I really wanted a job with this firm. When they kindly broke the news that they were hiring a more seasoned senior, I kept my cool but was crushed inside. It was my ideal job. I moped in my apartment for days until Jane, one of my dearest friends, called me from her car outside my house. She couldn't take it anymore; she said she would drive me around until I made the decision to get back on my horse and move on. Somewhere around mile 100, I realized I wasn't ready for that job. I was really young, and although I might have pulled it off, I would have been on such a learning curve that I would have been totally stressed and maybe unsuccessful. Maybe it wasn't the best for me. At that moment, sitting in a car in the middle of nowhere, I pretended that frustration, disappointment, and sadness were tangible things. I took them in my hands and rubbed them as if they were crumpled pieces of paper. Then I opened the window and pretended that I was throwing them into the wind. My friend thought I was crazy, but I told her what had just happened. We both realized I was free. I could now concentrate on gaining the experience I needed to land this ideal job. Two years later, the PR firm offered me a full-time position, but I had decided to move to the States and that was a life dream. A bigger dream.

Step 5: "What is my Intention?"

This is the phase where you can turn the original upset and pain around. You can design what you want instead. You can let go of the way you did something in the past. You can affirm a different choice. To formulate your intention, you are "forced" to clarify what really matters to you. By doing so, you set the new habit in motion. You announce to the Universe what you want, and that is a powerful force.

Diane decided to dedicate her upcoming vacation to designing her new life. She constructed her time in such a way that every day she would try a different angle. One day she did a collage of images that represented the life she wanted. She had pictures of a woman alone and blossoming. She had one of her grandfather, who was a reference point of kindness and tolerance. Another day, she lined up interviews with her married friends to explore the qualities they had in their marriages and those she could start thinking of that might be possible for her. She started a journal and covered pages with "forgiveness" statements. She was well on her way to recovery.

Step 6: Reap Your Reward

You wake up one morning, and somehow your chest feels less tight, more open. You experience a joy and a peace that are not familiar. There is a spring in your walk. It seems you found water in the desert. You feel like you can tackle some project you have never dared to. You might organize a trip, or ask your girlfriend to marry you. Or you might decide to get pregnant. Or you go and ask for that raise. Or you write a book. Or you just feel better in your skin. Sometimes it is a big, cathartic liberation; sometimes it is a quiet evening and you look out the window and you experience gratitude and warmth in your heart.

Diane is in this phase now. She is comfortable in her skin; she has cut her hair and wants me to introduce her to friends to potentially date. Through this difficult time of separation, she has gained great wisdom. When she starts a new relationship, it will be from a stronger place, a clearer and more deliberate place.

Forgiveness Is Not the Closing Act

It feels so good to forgive that we think it's the *end* of the process. The six steps to forgiveness are certainly an opportunity to move to the next level. You have forgiven yourself. You have forgiven others. Case closed.

Wait a second. Not exactly. This is a common mistake. Forgiveness does not work that way. Without learning from the past and taking action to correct it, which we'll be exploring in the next and last chapter, you will keep repeating the same mistake or a similar one, over and over. Read on.

Exercise	Here, we suggest no exercise. We recommend you enjoy the moment. Notice what has changed for you. Remember it can be subtle. Don't judge yourself for not having changed enough. (And if you do, forgive yourself!)

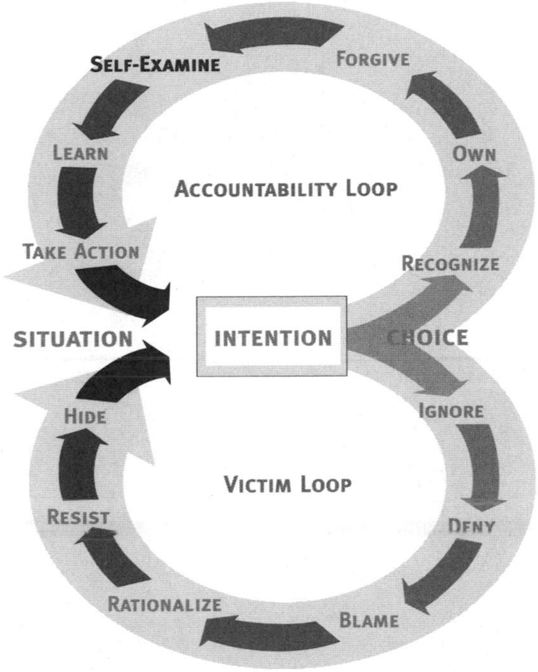
SELF-EXAMINE
FORGIVE
LEARN
OWN
ACCOUNTABILITY LOOP
TAKE ACTION
RECOGNIZE
SITUATION
INTENTION
CHOICE
HIDE
IGNORE
VICTIM LOOP
RESIST
DENY
RATIONALIZE
BLAME

CHAPTER SIX

The art of self-examination *is the turning point. From here, you can start creating your new life. It is in this phase that you gather information about next steps, reassess your situation, and make the choice to do something different than what you have done before.*

The Art of Self-Examination

"Problems cannot be solved at the same level of awareness that created them."
— **ALBERT EINSTEIN**

Let's face it: Your life is out of your control. The traffic you drive in, the weather, the laws you live under, no matter how much power or authority you have, you don't have control over a whole hell of a lot. And if that's not enough: You don't have control over *other people*.

What does this have to do with *accountability* and "*self-examination*"? It has to do with the one thing you *do* have control over—yourself. It is the one component you have total control over. Even when you don't have control over the circumstances of a particular situation, you always have a choice over your *reaction* to the situation. You have dominion over your thoughts and your beliefs. You have a choice of what you *remember* of the situation, over your *attitude*. That is ultimate power. That is probably what

73

guided the lives of Anne Frank and Nelson Mandela, what they were doing in their *minds* with the reality they were living in.

> "We cannot prevent birds from flying over our
> heads, but we can keep them from making nests
> on top of our heads."
> — **MARTIN LUTHER KING, JR.**

The Importance of Asking Questions

Asking a question opens a door, the door of possibilities, the door to new
solutions for old problems. A question allows you to tap into your creativity.
It stimulates your intuition. It gives you access to higher wisdom. It prepares
you to be surprised by an original idea. It is the soil of invention, innovation,
and discovery.

In contrast, if you *stop* asking questions, you shut doors. You can get
stuck in your ways, beliefs, and attitudes. You draw conclusions. You make
assumptions. You feel trapped because you don't see a way out. You think
you know it all, and that shuts down your ability to receive information
from your inner voice, others, or the Universe.

A few years ago, my twelve-year-old daughter came home from school
and asked for help on a writing assignment. My first reaction came from
the mind-set that I am a poor writer and couldn't help her. That self-
judgment shut the door on any possible solution. My second reaction was
a judgment of her. "Earlier, you wasted time talking on the phone and
watching TV. Now it's too late." This was another judgment, another closed
door. My daughter was stuck with her unsolved writing problem, and I
was stuck with my frustration.

Then I remembered what I teach: *ask questions*. Was she on the phone
simply to chat, or was she trying to get help from her friend? Am I really
a poor writer? Do I ever avoid a difficult assignment by crashing in front
of the TV? This opened up a creative flow. It made me feel compassionate, and I was able to reconnect with her and help her complete her
homework.

Exercise Take some time to think of a situation in which you felt stuck. Maybe it was at work dealing with your boss or a client. Or it might have been at home dealing with a spouse, a child, or a neighbor. Or it might pertain to travel plans or car problems. After each situation, ask yourself the following series of questions to see if the situation could have led to a different outcome:

■ Am I making an *assumption* about this situation?

■ What *judgments* am I placing against others or myself?

■ Do I know anyone who has *dealt successfully* with a similar situation?

■ What is the very first thing I can do to make some movement *right now*?

■ What *strength* do I have that can assist me in resolving this issue?

■ What is *a different way* I could be thinking about this?

Please send us questions that you find helpful to get unstuck!

E-mail us at questions@impaqcorp.com

Three Modes of Involvement

Now you are ready to ask the tough questions we already talked about in this book: *In what ways did you create, promote, or allow the current situation you are in?*

John Roger asks this question in his book *Life 101*. He recommends acknowledging that "you have *something* to do with what's happened. Even if you are not sure what that might be, ask yourself, 'If I did create, promote, or allow this, what might that be?'" The answer might surprise you:

■ If you are the *creator*, your behavior is a direct cause of the situation.

■ If you are a *promoter*, you're not directly causing the situation, but you're enabling or encouraging someone else to cause it.

■ If you are *an allower*, you're participating by *not* participating. By that we mean you're allowing the situation to continue by silently standing by and doing nothing to prevent it from happening.

Let's look at a common example that many families struggle with: the budget. Imagine that your objective is to balance your budget and to build your savings for future expenses, such as your kids' college education and your retirement. What is your current situation? You simply can't seem to make ends meet. On a consistent basis, your monthly bills outpace your income and you're not building your long-term savings.

If you ask "how am I contributing to the current situation?" and you are the one maxing out your credit cards, then say hello to the *creator* of the problem—you. If you find you're not spending the money yourself, but you've given your kids their own credit cards and encouraged your spouse to spend freely, look in the mirror and greet the great *promoter*—that would be you! Finally, even if you are the responsible spender, but you never speak up about how the rest of your family spends money, open your arms and welcome the one who *allows* the situation to happen—yes, you again.

Once you know how you are contributing to a situation, you need to explore that situation to an even greater degree, and learn as much as you can about the hows and whys of your involvement.

Digging Deeper for Answers

Figuring out how you created, promoted, or allowed a situation puts the focus on your physical actions. The first things you want to look at are your *behaviors*, the most obvious evidence of your personal involvement.

Often when you want to change a habit, you only change one aspect. You want to lose weight, so you eat less. You want to quit smoking, so you throw away the last pack in your pocket. Well, that is not enough. There is a lot that got you to overeat and smoke in the first place, and it takes deep self-examination to get to the root if you want to change the habit for good.

Let's take the example that you're not healthy because you eat too much. You jump into action and vow to get your weight under control. You try eating a little less each day; go on a crash diet; get hypnotized. And yet, you've succeeded in losing ten pounds, only to gain back fifteen. What's the problem?

The problem is that you haven't uncovered the *full extent* of your involvement in the situation. There are two elements of self-assessment that you have ignored: your *beliefs* and your *emotions*. They act like huge rubber bands that pull you right back into your old behaviors. Human behavior is supported and driven by beliefs and emotions. You have not yet figured out how your *thoughts* and *feelings* contribute to your eating habits.

Not only does it happen to individuals, but also to organizations and even countries. Companies often restructure, implement new technology, or adopt the latest improvement program. Countries legislate new fiscal or social policies. Very much like many people in weight loss programs, companies and governments will put forth a huge effort to change, only to be pulled right back to old patterns by the rubber-band effect.

I was called in to work with a management team of a federal agency. I met with Stan, the director of the department, to understand its history. The department's people had several initiatives that weren't getting accomplished. They had been working on the problem for several months, using a host of consultants. They thought that *lack of trust* was preventing them from attaining their objectives. So they hired a team-building consultant who used group games to help them work together. After the session, everyone was inspired and motivated.

For a while, everything improved, and people treated each other with great respect. Then, the workload increased, and they stopped being responsive. Information wasn't being shared, which caused some milestones to be missed, and they couldn't get the right people in the room to make a decision because they were too busy. This consultant had focused on the *emotional* arena. That was not enough. They went back to their old destructive behaviors. Rubber-band effect.

Stan called in a productivity consultant. He figured that the overwhelming workload was causing breakdowns in coordination, information sharing, and effective decision making. If managers were more organized, they would be less stressed and have more time to support one another, and that would prevent the relationship breakdowns. The work with this consultant assisted them individually, but it didn't help them to collaborate. This consultant had improved their *behavioral* competence. That was not enough. They moved back into a mode of protection, and it resulted in territorialism. Rubber-band effect.

When Stan called us, he was desperate. He was clear we were his last attempt. I explained the crucial importance of improving their belief, behavior, and emotional responses *at the same time*. Otherwise, the rubber-band effect was going to make them fail.

We started by creating a Vision of Leadership, where they described their "ideal state" of effectiveness as a unified team resolving problems and making decisions. This created a new mind-set by verbalizing a different picture. For the first time, they got a glimpse of real teamwork.

We invited the group to describe life in their department if they were living this vision. What would it look like and feel like? How would information be shared? How would they solve problems and conflicts? How would decisions be made? How would people behave in their meetings? How would the trust manifest? For example, they wrote:

> "Team members meet with customers at regular intervals to discuss expectations, form lasting partnerships, share information, elicit mutual support, and gain feedback on corporate performance."

They came up with a similar sentence that described the ideal state for each area of execution. Each got measured and was prioritized and tracked for improvement. This process addressed the *behavioral* change.

Finally, it became apparent that their inability to resolve conflict effectively was the root cause of their trust issue. I asked them to describe how they could resolve conflicts in an ideal way from that point on.

> "We could go to the person we have a problem with directly, instead of talking about it behind their backs. We could ask an agreed-upon third person to be present when a conflict arises, to help maintain the neutrality. We could commit to stay kind and not attack one another, by focusing on the issue, not the person."

This list of conditions was agreed upon by each team member. The team printed the agreement and displayed it on the wall of their meeting room. It got reviewed at each team meeting to keep it alive and present in each person's mind.

Six months later, the team had accomplished eight of their top ten initiatives. Their trust, communication, and support for each other improved 35 percent, according to measurements established prior to the start of our work. They continued those improvements for the next three years, until the department was reorganized. Once they addressed the *beliefs*, *emotions*, and the *behavior*, they could sustain the desired changes.

Let's look at each of these factors in more detail.

Belief

A belief is a mental state made of our mind-set, assumptions, and convictions. It influences our attitude, behaviors, and choices. Walt Disney once said, "If you can dream it, you can do it." That belief manifested a radical transformation in the way people experience entertainment and fun. Similarly, the group of people at the federal agency first needed to see themselves as a team and commit to it. Not just getting along, but being interdependent. They couldn't succeed without the support of each other.

Emotions

Emotions are the feelings that trigger our reactions. Charles Schwab said, "A man can succeed at almost anything for which he has unlimited enthusiasm." Emotions are the engine behind the self-confidence and trust you need to get up and go.

The opposite is also true. If approached with discouragement and doubt, you can fail at the simplest tasks. The team at the federal agency had emotional distress because they avoided dealing with their unresolved conflict. They needed a structure to address conflicts. It wasn't enough to just be sensitive and understanding of their differences. They needed to create a *process* to resolve conflict.

Behaviors

Behaviors depict the way we conduct ourselves and are the actions that produce results. Benjamin Disraeli said, "Action may not always bring happiness, but there is no happiness without action." Ultimately, it's the improvement of your *behavior* that enables you to reach excellence. The federal agency team created common practices for developing teamwork and accomplishing their initiatives.

You might have heard that the definition of insanity is doing the same thing over and over and expecting a different result. Well, the same holds true with your thoughts, feelings, and beliefs. If you keep repeating the same thoughts that trigger the same feelings and keep functioning from the same set of beliefs that got you where you are, you are going to keep creating the same reality around you. It's critical to ask questions and examine the relationship between your mind-set, emotions, and behavior.

Consider this example. Sue worked in a nursing unit as a supervisor when the head manager position became open. That was her dream job, but she didn't get it. It was a big disappointment when one of the nurses who reported to her, Donna, got the position instead. Sue was livid. She was more experienced and had been committed to the organization for a longer period of time. It was unfair. In her mind-set, she should have gotten the job. She understandably felt angry and hurt. It grew into open resentment, and that emotional state prevented her from functioning in the team. Finally, she started isolating herself from the group and that escalated into rebellion and resistance. Sue was doing the minimum just to get by. She even made derogatory comments about her new boss. It was getting ugly.

Donna contacted me to see if I could coach Sue to accept the change. Donna really liked Sue and wanted her to stay on the team, but only if she could accept the new situation. When I met with Sue, it was clear that she felt undermined by upper management. I agreed that it was an unusual move, but asked if it changed her intention to serve her patients and the doctors. I asked her if she still cared about the other nurses. She replied that her caring hadn't changed. She was still committed to contributing as much as she could.

This conversation helped her get back in touch with the original mind-set that had gotten her the supervisor position in the first place. Sue also said it changed her belief that she would ever become a manager. I asked her if she was sure she wanted to be the head nurse of the department. She was clear about that.

So I assisted her in seeing this next period as a time to prepare for rising to a head nurse position. Sue asked management for clarity about what she needed to improve to get that position. She also asked her friend, Betsy, a head nurse in another department, for advice. Sue said she might even be open to inviting Donna for lunch, so she could ask to get trained in what she was lacking. Sue now had *a new mind-set* that reflected her true dream once again. She also had *a plan of action*. She began modifying her behavior and was back on track.

She mentioned that she still felt disappointed about not getting the job. Disappointment only comes when expectations are not fulfilled. She felt the job was owed to her, and that is a mind-set that often leads to disappointment. I invited her to look at the situation in a way that was going to support her. What if she was not ready for this job? What if another department also needed a head nurse, and she was better qualified for that department? What if management had decided to promote her to an even better salary, and they needed to wait a couple of months before it could happen? This series of questions allowed her to change her expectation and focus on what she needed to do to achieve her intention.

The name of the game was to do what she needed to do to get the job, but also to be able to let go and trust that a greater opportunity was coming her way if she didn't get it. Sue's failure to get the job could also mean that she needed more expertise or more experience for the position. Either way, she could get up and get ready.

I checked in with Donna a year later. Sue was promoted six months after we had this coaching session into a head nurse position and was doing great.

Avoid Going on Automatic Pilot

Thinking, doing, and/or feeling the same thing over and over is part of what I call the *automatic pilot syndrome*. If your unexplored mind-sets or emotions are driving your behaviors, then stand up and greet this syndrome. Frankly, sometimes it's not a bad syndrome to have, if your habits are healthy. For example, when I get up in the morning, put toothpaste on my toothbrush, brush my teeth, then take a shower, my automatic pilot is serving me quite well. The problem arises when I come home from work and find myself mysteriously opening the refrigerator without even having a thought of being hungry. Or pouring a glass of vodka. Or taking pain medication to numb the stress accumulated. My automatic pilot switch has been flipped on, and it isn't a good one. What should I do at this point?

First, I need to *recognize* that the automatic pilot switch is "ON." Immediately after, I need to ask myself if having it ON is *serving* me or *hurting* me. In this case, it looks like this: Is eating in excess when I'm not hungry serving me, or is it hurting me? Is pouring myself a vodka right now serving or hurting me? Is the medication serving or hurting? Once I know the answer, I am able to make a *choice* again. A real one, not an out of control, impulsive choice. A choice that is deliberate and fits in my bigger goals of being healthy and aware.

Balancing Your Life Equations

As you get closer to making decisions or setting forth a new direction or a change, your risk increases—will it be the right decision? Do you want to be involved in that new effort, which could fail? Is this in your best interest? Suddenly, a lot of time spent analyzing a situation could turn into emotional turmoil based on fear, anxiety, or even enthusiasm. How many times have you made a decision or taken a course of action only to ask yourself later, "What was I thinking?"

If emotion or confusion takes over, a way to handle it is with a simple cost/benefit analysis. Using this approach, you brainstorm as many costs and benefits of making the desired/proposed change and the costs and benefits of not making the desired/proposed change. You can use this same approach when there is more than one option. Reviewing this list may result in immediate clarity. But if it doesn't, there is one more activity: identify the costs that you can *influence*. The more you can influence, the better your alternatives.

Don, a manager of the training department for a telecommunications company in Northern California, called me with a dilemma. A task force within his team of managers developed a new process for enrolling employees into their program. But when it was introduced to the entire team, some of them rejected the idea. One particular person liked the current process and thought this new method would be too hard for employees to implement. Polarization took place in the team, where half thought the change was an improvement, and the other half thought employees wouldn't accept the change.

Don believed in the change but wanted to respect other people's opinions. They already had spent three weekly meetings on the subject, and he was losing his cool. I recommended a cost/benefit analysis, for both the option of implementing the change and for the option of staying with the current process. Then compare the lists to discover which process would be more effective and would accomplish the goals.

Don had another meeting with his team in thirty minutes. An hour later, he called me back and was laughing. "We did it, we looked over the lists, and it was so clear. Nobody could deny the value of implementing the change. Even the naysayers are on board." The new process was not only sound, but the list of costs associated with it could be addressed. Even the fear of employees not being able to implement it was solved by an idea of training that came in the brainstorm. As a result of using this cost/benefit analysis, Don was able to resolve this three-week problem in less than sixty minutes with his team.

Similarly, I once had a colleague, Jana, who smoked and couldn't quit. She was incredibly smart and knew about the health dangers of smoking. But still, those weren't enough of a reason for her to quit. So, we examined the costs and benefits of her smoking habit.

"How does smoking serve you?" I asked.

"It helps me in social situations," she replied. How else? "It calms my nerves in tense or emotional circumstances." How else? "It helps me keep my weight down. I eat more when I don't smoke." We continued the drill until we had all the ways in which smoking served her.

Then I asked Jana about the *costs*. She had a list: health risks, financial cost, smelly clothes, the usual stuff. How else? She named a few more costs. How else? I insisted. For a moment she stopped and thought and then she suddenly exclaimed, "Oh my God, my smoking is a wall. It's a barrier between me and other people. Smoking costs me closeness in relationships." When she got close with someone, she would always take out a cigarette. The conversation would drift to something safer, less vulnerable. She shared her intention of deepening her ability to be close to her friends, even a boyfriend. In fact, her last boyfriend used to complain about how much she smoked. She thought it was because he didn't like smoking. But, looking back she could see the separation it created in their communication, by breaking off deep conversations so she could go outside for a smoke. She never saw how her smoking was related to her fear of intimacy.

Jana realized that smoking was undermining her hopes for finding a life partner. That realization, coming from a relatively short list of costs and benefits, became the impetus to quit smoking.

With a clear, new awareness of the costs and benefits of your behaviors, successful transitions can be made. You've moved from the *preparation* phases of your work by exploring, recognizing, owning, forgiving, and self-examining. We are now ready to move into the solution phases of *learning* and *taking action*.

We are getting closer to achieving our goals. In the next chapter, we'll begin to convert the insights we've garnered into *learning*.

Exercise   Find a friend to ask you the following questions. The only rule is that he or she can't give you any advice or pass any judgment. However, your friend can repeat a question if he or she feels you can go deeper in your response. The goal is to go as deep as you can and get the most out of this exercise.

1. What is one aspect of your behavior, attitude, or performance that you would like to improve?

2. When does it show up as a problem in your life?

3. How do you create, promote, or allow this problem to continue?

4. How does it benefit you to *not* improve this issue?

5. What does it *cost* you to not improve this issue?

6. What could you do differently to be more effective?

7. What support would you like from others?

8. What is the next small action you can take and when will you take it?

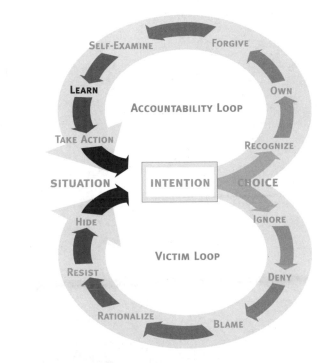

CHAPTER SEVEN

Be a master learner. *Seize the opportunity and let yourself be transformed. Think differently. Integrate a new behavior that serves your purpose. If what you did in a previous situation didn't work out, the process of learning guarantees you will proceed differently next time. It might take a few tries, but eventually you will hit your mark.*

chapter | **seven**

Be a Master Learner

"Change is the end result of all true learning."

— **LEO BUSCAGLIA**

In the last chapter, you gathered information about your mind-sets, emotions, and behaviors. This process is much like a doctor who asks questions that give him context and history so he can make a diagnosis. You have done the same thing with yourself. It is now time, in this chapter, to *learn* from the answers you have discovered.

Everyone has his or her own style of learning. Whether you are an introvert or an extrovert, whether you're three or seventy-three years old, from India or Manhattan, whether your approach to learning is mental or emotional, there are as many styles of learning as there are DNAs. I'm not going to attempt to explore them all in this book. Instead, we are going to focus on *keys* for learning, so you can be prepared to take action.

Learning as a Change Agent

Learning is only interesting if it generates a change. You may want to change a habit, an awareness, a skill, or some intellectual ability you have. Learning is only helpful if knowing this new information improves your world. It makes you laugh; adds culture or perspective; makes you kinder, wiser, more effective; or allows you to make better decisions, or help someone else in some way. It impacts you. And from that added learning, you are different.

Learning Can Bring Good or Bad News

If someone spends time in prison and discovers new ways of robbing a bank, that person has learned something new, and he or she is certainly transformed—but not for the better.

Learning has to come hand in hand with *positive* intentions. Will it improve the life of your community, the company you work for, your clients, your children, your coworkers? Will it make you a better human being? Personally, I like to keep in mind the highest good of all concerned when I go about my day.

Traps that Prevent Learning

We say we want to learn, but do we really? I often encounter people who seem committed to their growth, but who get caught in their own stumbling blocks—their emotional, mind-set, or behavioral habits. Arthur was an experienced internal consultant for a large manufacturing organization. I was coaching him on the accountability methodology. We always finished our sessions on a high note with great progress. But every time we would start again, I would have the same surprise. He was not *retaining* what we had covered.

At first, I couldn't put my finger on his pattern. Arthur was motivated and had academic degrees to illustrate his ability to learn. I started noticing how often he said, "I get it, I understand." He was getting it, but only intellectually. He was not *integrating* it in a way that improved his abilities. He was gaining new information but was not learning. Learning was impossible because he stayed on the surface of the information and was not letting the learning transform into *application*.

I had coached another associate who reminded me of Arthur. Virginia also always said "I get it, I understand." In her case, she didn't. She was so ashamed of acknowledging she didn't understand something, she had developed the reflex of saying "I understand" when she really didn't. In her case, learning was impossible. To learn, you need the openness and the courage to know that you do not know everything.

We've identified six traps that get in the way of true learning.

Trap #1: Attachment to the Old Way

There is comfort in the familiar. People caught in this trap cling to their current reality and feel threatened by new approaches. Sometimes it's the fear of failure, but many times it's simply, "I don't want to make the effort to learn something new."

A few months ago, a small printing company hired me to help its production manager to optimize his space in preparation for the growth of the company. I was struck by the manager's habits. He was almost *proud* to tell me how the place had not changed in the last three years. He had his process down. He did one job at a time. All of the supplies were kept in one part of the large room. It was clear that if efficiencies were to be improved, he would need to handle multiple jobs at the same time. He would also need to move his supplies closer to the equipment where those supplies were used. Although he was willing to move the supplies, he was not willing to change his process. Within six months, management replaced him with another production manager, who modified the process to handle multiple jobs—and productivity increased by 35 percent.

Trap #2: "It Won't Work Here: We Are Different"

Many people want to feel unique and special. In an organization, they don't like the idea that what has worked in another organization would fit in their own, because they feel that they are different.

A few years ago, I was consulting for a division of a South American petroleum company that was implementing new technology. We first established a clear vision for the use of the new technology involving all of the departments affected. Using our accountability approach, we focused more on developing "recovery" plans rather than attempting to shoot for perfection. Finally, we developed success factors for the implementation process, which were tracked and measured. We planned this effort in six months and began implementation. It was uncomfortable for people of the division, because the workers in that division were accustomed to slower change, but they moved through their resistance and achieved results within one year and improved morale by 25 percent at the same time.

Another division within the company was implementing the same technology and asked me to present our accountability-based approach. However, they chose a different approach, affirming that they were more sophisticated than the other division. They planned for perfection and waited for buy-in. A year later, they attempted to implement the same change, only to be stopped by resistance. They created more task forces to study the problem and began implementing six months later, which was *twelve months after* the other division had completed the change.

Although it is true that we are unique, there are some commonalities that make us the same. We all have pain, fear, and thoughts. It is important to keep your need for individuality in the right place, when it comes to inventing new products, or expressing yourself artistically. But it is also important to stay *open* to receiving knowledge from proven sources.

Trap #3: "We Tried It Before"

Experience is a powerful teacher, especially when the lesson involves pain. "We don't want *that* to happen again." It is easy to move into resistance when you've had a previous bad experience.

A while back, I was preparing to write my master's thesis when my computer crashed. I was stuck. My friend Robert suggested I use a handheld recorder. However, I had tried to use one in the past, and every time I would freeze. I would stare at the recorder and say a lot of "ah's." I was never able to get into the flow of sharing my thoughts freely. I responded, "I have tried it before and was never successful."

Robert patiently asked me when the last time I gave it a try was. I said it was about a year ago. He said, "Great, then you can give it a try again and see if anything has changed."

I argued a little more saying, "Well, I haven't developed my skills in talking into a recorder."

He quickly responded, "Maybe not, but you have participated in personal growth workshops, resulting in some major changes in your life, including the development of your company, resolving issues with your parents, and healing some old emotional wounds."

I decided to give it a try. In one weekend, I was able to dictate my thesis of eighty pages into my new hand-held recorder with ease. I was surprised at the difference, but Robert explained that with all the other changes in my life, my confidence had increased and had made it possible for me to now be successful with the hand-held recorder.

People change. Things change. Society changes. You can't hold what happened in the past and make it the gospel truth. So try again. Give it another shot.

There is a story about an elephant that is tied to a wall by a heavy chain when it is a baby. It is just too small to break the big chain. As the elephant grows up, its handlers replace the heavy chain with a lighter chain. Still, when the elephant tries to break free, it feels the chain tugging at the wall and gives up. Eventually, its handlers replace the chain with a wire. Finally, by the time the elephant is fully grown, all it needs is a thin rope to tie it to the wall. Yes, the elephant could easily break the rope, but it no longer had the belief that breaking the rope would lead to freedom.

You should always challenge what you've been doing for years. What worked before might not be the best solution anymore.

Trap #4: "It Wasn't Invented Here"

This might be an issue of control or ego. I have seen this syndrome with managers who wouldn't accept an idea from their direct reports until it was presented as their own ideas. I've also seen parents taking credit for an idea their child came up with. And I've seen organizations that would not accept a tool from a consultant because the organization's full-time staff didn't create that tool.

I recently worked with a senior management team for a clothing retail chain. I had been teaching the principles of accountability to their managers for a couple of weeks, when they started receiving feedback that they were more focused in team meetings, more open to collaborating cross-functionally, and more effectively prioritizing their projects and tasks. They seemed to respect my approach. Even the skeptics seemed convinced that it was going to bring positive change.

Given that success, I invited them to use a project management form that I had developed over the past twenty years. That, they refused. They wanted to make up their own form. One of their assistants has kept me informed that they have implemented five different management forms in three months but none has worked for them. They are stuck.

I believe in trying something and finding out whether it works for you. I hope that is what you do with this book. Check it out. Try it on for size. Decide if any of it works for you.

Trap #5: "I Have to Label It"

When people hear a new concept, they sometimes feel the need to put it in a box they are familiar with. For example, almost every time I present the Personal Accountability Model I use in this book, someone comes up and tells me it is from Alcoholics Anonymous, or the Torah, or the Koran, or whatever scripture they read. Or it sounds like Maslow's hierarchy of needs, or some variation of that. Although most of the time this is flattering, sometimes people use this trap to demonstrate that my approach isn't valid. In other words, they believe they have seen it before, in another form, and they tell me it didn't work.

A regional health system in Canada had a goal of changing the culture of healthcare within the regional area. Overseeing a health system that is socialized and government funded, the organization employs about 28,000 people. It has been committed to improving the care for patients as well as the environment for employees ever since the health system was regionalized five years ago. The organization's interest in accountability grew from its Department of Organization Development and Wellness.

However, it was clear from my first assignment that the system would not mandate organizations within its regional system to use our accountability systems. Accountability would be implemented as a "grass roots" effort that the system would help fund and support.

In the first six months, almost 1800 people in this organization have been exposed to our accountability practices, including trainings, leadership team-working sessions, and certification programs.

People are excited about the positive impact it has already had. One hospital improved its success factors of performance execution by 81 percent—of which 46 percent was significant in the first four months.

Labeling anything is probably the biggest waste of time of any of these traps. Accountability is dedicated to finding what works. When it stops working, stop using it and find a better way, regardless of what you call it. When people don't like the word "accountability," I ask them what word they want to use, because it isn't the *word* that will get them results but the *action* related to this process.

Trap #6: "Prove It to Me"

Some people can't try anything new, or even accept the validity of a new approach if it can't be proved.

Matt, the manager of educational services at a major teaching hospital in Houston, asked me to make a presentation to John, his director of organizational development. Matt experienced major improvements in his previous hospital when I worked with managers to improve cross-functional teamwork. He was convinced that we could address the territorialism that existed within his new organization.

When I presented our methodology to John, it was clear that he was skeptical. He immediately asked for proof that our team system and accountability technology worked. I shared with him the results of several healthcare organizations, including some that were teaching hospitals. Matt shared his experience in the meeting as well. But John was still resistant. He said, "No, I want to understand the *theories* that are the basis of your work." I told him the basis of my work involved an integration of many theories of leadership including Maslow, Lawler, Margulies, Blanchard, and Lewin. However, the true methodology comes from my being a practitioner. John was not impressed, and my client references and previous history of getting measurable results made no difference. There was nothing I could have done to prove it to him.

Proof is helpful, but it's not the only way to make decisions. Experience and intuition are essential components.

We Choose What We Learn

Like everything we have talked about in this book, accountability gets you to watch carefully what gets in your psyche. Learning is no exception. You *choose* what you let in. You *choose* what you study. You have a responsibility as to what you teach yourself that is similar to what you teach your children. What do you teach yourself? And when you are taught beliefs that are not serving you or the greater good, you have an *accountability* to eliminate the learnings that are pulling you down, that are polluting the air.

> "The first problem for all of us, men and women,
> is not to learn, but to unlearn."
> **— GLORIA STEINEM**

Please, Leave Your Ego at the Door

To enter the classroom where most learning occurs—life—I recommend checking your attitude at the door. Come in humble and open to discovering what you don't know, or to rediscovering what you thought you knew. To be a master learner, you should believe you know nothing, and you should be willing to go back to the drawing board every day. There are a lot of blessings showered on the innocent one. Empty your bowl of rice before you start each day, to see what the day has to bring.

New Tricks for an Old Dog

We hired Michael with the expectation of him becoming a senior consultant. He had more experience than the rest of us, including me. He discovered us when we had the same client, an insurance company on the West Coast. The results we achieved with the client in areas of customer service and cost containment outpaced all of the other change efforts in the organization. Michael was impressed with our results and intrigued about our accountability methodology. He approached us seeking a position.

As we started teaching Michael our strategies and tools, he had a major challenge. He was smart and quick; that was not the problem. But he was not open to learning anything new. He kept comparing everything I presented to him to his old techniques. His methods were well founded in organizational development theory, and he had been using them for more than twenty years. He kept trying to fit our models into his old framework and they didn't connect. The basis of his methodologies and our accountability approach were in conflict.

I finally asked him to forget everything he knew and approach our techniques with fresh eyes. His assignment was to redirect his reflexes and stop himself from the habit of comparing new information to the old. I asked him to be the student, not the expert. His ego couldn't take it. Even if he demonstrated some interest in our approach, he was resistant, acting like he knew it all and had nothing to learn. We eventually parted ways when it became evident we were not going to be able to find a satisfying working relationship.

TAKING WISDOM FROM INSIDE AND OUT

The last few years of tennis great André Agassi's career are a vivid example of how lessons can come from a multitude of sources. Agassi was the world's top-ranked tennis player in April 1995. By November 1997 he had fallen to number 141. And then, in a nineteen-month effort, he returned to the top spot, finishing number one in the 1999 season.

The comeback was fueled by wisdom drawn from internal and external sources. Internally, Agassi came to some critical realizations about his career. The most important was that he truly wanted to return to the highest echelons of tennis. "This is my time," he said to personal trainer Gil Reyes (as reported by Michael Perry of *The Cincinnati Enquirer*). "If I don't do it now, I'll regret it so much. That's what it's all about, eh, Gil? No regrets?"

Agassi also learned how to overcome his *internal barriers* to success. "The obstacles are not impossibilities anymore," explained Reyes. "André has told me so many times, he used to be afraid of fear, but now he realizes that the more scared he gets, the harder he's going to fight. Now it's all business."

For external wisdom, Agassi looked to two longtime sources of support: trainer Reyes and tennis coach Brad Gilbert. It was Gilbert who taught his student strategy. "I think he brought a real element of thinking out there on the court," said Agassi. "I'm always aware of what it is I'm doing and what it is that's going on. I'm using that as a huge weapon." Reyes created the physical lessons that supported the comeback bid. And, even he was surprised by the energy Agassi put into the weight training and running regime.

Looking back at his subsequent re-ascension to the heights of tennis in mid-2000, Agassi told reporter Perry, "Knocking those questions down one by one, and fighting your obstacles and battles one by one, it's given me a strength and a peace that I am just overwhelmed with."

Let the Learning Come from You

There is an incredible wisdom within ourselves that we tend to forget because we are so accustomed to looking for answers outside of ourselves—from the Internet, television, training, books by experts. These are all around us, so much so that our inner voice can get a little lost in all the chaos. I know because I have a team at play inside myself, and I have learned to listen to its voices and use them to teach me what I need to learn. Meet my team:

- The *critic* is demanding. He teaches me to never quit, to expect a lot of myself, and to deliver the most impeccable work.

- The *higher self* connects me to the Universe. He teaches me to trust what is to come and who is to come.

- The *rebel* reminds me to question what's established. She teaches me to challenge rules that might not work anymore.

- The *creative* inspires me to look for different solutions, to look upside down and inside out, just to see if there is another way.

- The *scared* protects me. He is the one to remind me to wear a parachute if I am jumping out of a plane.

- The *inner child* pouts, whines, reminds me to take a nap, or go play with the butterflies.

The awareness that I have a team inside of me is fairly recent, but I take comfort in knowing they are on my side. For the longest time, I couldn't stand being alone; it felt so dark in there. If anything, that team felt like an enemy. My critic censured me; my higher self sounded "new agey" and, frankly, a little weird; my rebel dyed my hair purple; my creative was angry and frustrated; my scared stopped me from taking any risk; and my inner child was mad at me and force-fed me chocolate cake for not hearing her voice. Not so fun.

Who Is Coming For Dinner?

The learning occurs if I am able to observe who shows up where and what environment seems to trigger what team player. When I go to a meeting at the office, I tend to give the floor to my critic. One of my assistants seems to give total power to her inner child. She is a powerful woman, but somehow in meetings she sounds like she is seven years old. I have learned to ask for her opinion, which I highly value, before we enter the meeting room. I just would never get it if I asked her once the meeting had started.

Learning Is What We Take With Us

It sometimes takes a dramatic event to force us to realize what matters most to us. "Locked-in syndrome" is a condition where the body shuts down entirely, except the blink of the left eye. The brain and the mental abilities stay intact. Following a car crash, Jean Dominique Bauby, editor at *Elle* magazine, was diagnosed with this condition. He dictated a book before he died using a cumbersome code based on the blink of his eye. One blink, yes; two blinks no; three A; four B . . .

"Left with nothing, what I have learned matters so much more" were his last words.

Recognizing, owning, forgiving, self-examining, and learning have gotten us to the door of accountability. The door to freedom. The door to a deliberate life. In the next chapter, we will look at the last step in the accountability model: taking action. What are we going to do and how can we be deliberate in what we choose as our next physical move?

> "To know others is wisdom, to know yourself is enlightenment."
>
> **— LAO TZU**

Exercise   **INTEGRATE YOUR DISCOVERIES**

Part 1: Be the Scientist

1. List five different lessons you have learned from reading this book. This can include awareness about yourself and your relationships with others, new strategies for being successful, or fresh approaches for making changes in your life.

2. Identify any patterns between your five lessons:

   ■ Is there a common theme?

   ■ Do they focus on a particular area (mindset, emotions, behaviors)?

   ■ Are there environmental conditions that link to these lessons?

3. What are your conclusions? What actions can you take for improvement?

Part 2: Keep a Journal

Take time to list what you learned at the end of every day. This can be a five-minute or more exercise that becomes your encyclopedia of personal wisdom. Then, once a month, take time to review what you have written during the month. Notice what has changed in your life and what you still want to improve.

Self-Examine
Forgive
Learn
Own
Accountability Loop
Take Action
Recognize
SITUATION
INTENTION
CHOICE
Hide
Ignore
Victim Loop
Resist
Deny
Rationalize
Blame

CHAPTER EIGHT

Take action. *There is a direct relationship between your life as a whole and all the actions you take every hour of every day. To like your life, the sum of your actions, you have to like each action individually. And it is easier to take smaller steps than big ones.*

chapter **eight**

Take Action

"Even if you are on the right track, you
will get run over if you just sit there."
— **WILL ROGERS**

Nothing you have read in this book is worth even the cost of the
paper it is printed on if you don't *take action* on what you have learned.

The final and irrevocable reality is this: As important as ownership,
self-awareness, and learning are in the achievement of your dreams, they
won't get you anywhere in and of themselves. But *action* will.

Take a Step, Any Step

It doesn't matter if you take a wrong step, but the surest way to fail reaching your goals is to remain in place. The minute you stop moving, you
ruin the chance of reaching your final destination. On the other hand, if
you're in motion, whether it is forward, sideways, or even backward, success simply becomes a matter of navigation.

Accountability does not exist without action. Remember the definition: *Accountability is taking action consistent with our desired outcomes.* You can't remove "taking action" from the equation. No action = no accountability.

Taking Action Has Powerful Benefits

The first benefit of action occurs *internally*. The more you act, the more you learn about whatever you are doing. You initiate a momentum. This enhanced level of experience builds your confidence in your capabilities and your trust in yourself.

The first time I para-sailed on skis I experienced a dramatic difference before and during the jump. When I was just *thinking* about it, I was scared. But once I was up there *flying*, I was relaxed and happy. For years, I had skied near the para-sailing school, hoping one day I would summon the courage to have a go at it. I judged myself for not doing it. I pretended I really didn't want to para-sail. I was so scared. Then one day, I had had enough of wishing. Almost in a robotic manner, I signed up, paid, listened to the instructor, put my helmet on, took a deep breath, and went for it. What a moment that was! The silence up there. The amazing experience of flying like an eagle. Writing about it now, I still feel the rush. I felt the reward of defying my fear. In that one second from inaction to action, I was *free*.

I consulted with the CEO and owner of an import-export company a few years ago. Lawrence was successful but somehow seemed unhappy with his accomplishments. One evening after a session with his team, I went back to the boardroom to get my coat. He was sitting there, alone in the dark. I felt compelled to sit with him. After a few minutes of silence I said, "You don't seem excited about your business anymore." He wasn't.

He started telling me about sculpting and what he felt when his hands were in clay and how, as a college student, he could stay up all night, molding and scraping. He had dreamt of being a sculptor all his life. Instead, his life had been swallowed by a family business and other people's expectations. He hadn't touched a tool for the past fifteen years. Our session had triggered feelings about abandoning an important part of himself. He had never had the courage to take the leap. I suggested taking it one step at a time and complete one action. One small action toward his passion. He could find his tools in the basement. He could sign up for a sculpting class and go on weekends. He could buy some clay and set up a table in his house.

That was three years ago. Lawrence now has a studio in the basement of his office and uses it every chance he has. I just received an invitation to a gallery opening in London. That's the power of taking one action, one small action at a time.

This is the choice we are making on the accountable path of self-development. Once you make the choice and overcome your fear, you develop the confidence to take on bigger challenges. By accepting that *you alone* are accountable for your own success, happiness, and self-fulfillment, you realize that *you alone* can build the courage and the drive to go after what you want to achieve.

Action also builds other people's trust in you. When you take action—even if you don't always fully accomplish your goals—you prove that you're willing to accept challenges and try new things. *You* become the one who *gets things done*. Lawrence became a model for those daring to take risks and for those wanting to improve their quality of life. He started a program called "One Step at a Time" where employees can take up to two hours a week to feed their dreams. Some people took up dance lessons; some learned a new language; some went home early to be with their kids.

Your willingness to act also helps others break through the barriers of fear. Once they see *you* take action, they will find the courage to do the same. In Lawrence's weekly meeting, the staff spends the last ten minutes sharing about their progress on "One Step at a Time" and deciding what the next small action could be to move forward.

Sometimes you need to take the lead, as Lawrence did, to show other people how to be courageous. From the time I was ten years old, my friends and I went ice-skating every winter at a lake near my house. One time, my cousins, Bob and Sue, came to visit and I invited them to come along—but once we got to the lake, they refused to go out on the ice. I understood their *initial* reluctance. They were afraid of falling through, but I didn't understand why they didn't trust me once I assured them that the lake froze solid every year, and that I had already been out on it safely several times that winter.

I finally realized no explanation was going to convince them. So I left them at the edge and skated to the middle of the lake: once they saw that the ice was solid, they skated out to join me—and we had a great day. My willingness to *take action* without them inspired them. I grew closer to both of them that winter. That action helped us build some trust in each other. It wasn't until years later that I realized how powerful taking action can be: how putting yourself out there—sometimes literally—can kick-start a project at work, at home, anywhere.

Three Obstacles to Action

We have identified three main obstacles to action: fear, internal resistance, and the trap of perfectionism. The first step to overcoming them is to understand what they are and how each of these traps works to get in your way of achieving success.

Obstacle #1: Fear

Fear is the biggest obstacle to action, and in a sense, it's also the basis for the other two. Anytime you face the unknown or attempt an action that you've never accomplished before, fear enters the picture. The closer you get to your goals, the closer you get to your fear of failure *and* your fear of success. In either case, you are going to experience change—and change can be scary.

Laura worked as the HR director of a large computer manufacturer. She was given a project to implement a new compensation plan, and it was due in six months. She thought that was enough time and was quite relaxed about it. By the end of the third month, though, pressure was building, and she began to realize that the job was more complex than she had originally thought. She started having a queasy feeling in the pit of her stomach. And then, seemingly instantaneously, there was only one month left. The stress of the fast-approaching deadline was now enormous. She was frantically wondering how she could have been so stupid as to think it was enough time. How could she get out of this mess? The fear was rising and getting in the way of making it happen.

Obstacle #2: Internal Resistance

Internal resistance builds as you get closer to your goals. As you approach your desired outcome, you become aware of all of the necessary work it will take to get there. At this point, you realize that you can't just *talk* about the actions you're going to take someday in the future; you must actually *take* those actions.

The difference between the many physically gifted people who dream of playing professional football and those who actually go on to play in the pros lies in their behaviors. If you want to reach the level of athletic ability needed to play pro ball, there are many non-negotiable behaviors. Every step you take toward going pro involves more work. You need to train hard and get into peak condition before you can even try out for a team.

This can feel like prison, particularly if you make sacrifices for something that you have no guarantee of actually getting. The natural response is to resist. If you put in minimal effort, you will have lost nothing if you don't get what you're after. If you can overcome and do all that is required of you to reach your goal, the result is not imprisonment but the freedom that comes from accomplishing and living your dreams.

I grew up with a guy who was a natural athlete. Jim was the best high school player in every sport he signed up for—a baseball pitcher, a football quarterback, and a point guard playing basketball. His love was basketball, so as a sophomore in high school, he set his sights only on playing basketball. He was the starting guard on the varsity basketball team, which won the district championship. For the next two years, he broke the record for the number of points he made in a game and the number of assists he made. He had the peripheral vision of a Magic Johnson and the grace to match. By the end of his high school career, he had received an offer to play for UCLA, the top university basketball team at that time, under the direction of Coach John Wooden.

Unfortunately, Jim never showed up for his meeting with Coach Wooden or for practice. He was having too much fun enjoying his summer break. He never had to work that hard for his skill. He had natural talent. Once his window of opportunity closed, it never reopened. He is remembered as the one who "could have been" a star.

Most of us aren't trying to become star basketball players, but we do have goals related to our careers and our families. If we don't continue to put the effort into achieving our goals by taking action, learning from our mistakes, and taking action again, we are giving up on ourselves. If we find *resistance* surfacing, it is important to ask questions to discover what the resistance is about. Is it fear of failure or success? Is it still your real intention and desire? Is there a skill that you are missing that is preventing you from going after your dreams? Do you need to just take action to get your energy started and move on your goal again? Do you need a coach or friend to assist you in staying on track until you become self-motivated again? You can ask questions about your beliefs, emotions, and behaviors to determine what needs changing and make the necessary adjustments.

Obstacle #3: Seeking Perfectionism

The trap of perfectionism is the third obstacle to action. Too often, we believe we must perform an action perfectly in order to succeed. If we can't be perfect, we do the one thing that dooms our efforts to failure: *we don't act*.

The truth is that action is not about perfection. This is a point that is often missed in business situations. Managers often believe that in order to succeed, everything must go like clockwork. So they spend inordinate amounts of time analyzing and planning and trying to take into account every possible factor in a project. Two things happen: either they never take action, or by the time they are finally ready to act, it's too late. For example, someone might lose an interesting ad campaign because he perfected it for so long that the client changed to an agency that could deliver faster. Or someone else might be working on a presentation of the results of her medical research, but she takes so long to make the charts in color and work her presentation to perfection that she actually arrives late to the meeting.

The ability to plan and execute anything flawlessly on the first try is a matter of sheer luck. And that is fine, because you're not aiming to be perfect. Your intention is to reach your goal, and you will soon see that there are proven ways to do exactly that.

RECOGNIZING FEAR

In one of my psychology classes, we were asked to select a life-changing project. There were two conditions: the dream had to be a big enough stretch; and if you didn't finish the project, you couldn't graduate.

One classmate, a shy and not very coordinated fellow, said he wanted to learn ballroom dancing. Our instructors allowed it, but suggested he raise the bar as much as he could.

Each one of us hit the wall of fear. What mattered is not that we hit the wall, but how we reacted when we hit it.

Some quit. *This has nothing to do with psychology, the professors are stupid*, blah, blah, blah. Others decided to start again. They went back and did the easy part. And hit the wall at the same place. Others abandoned their projects and picked another. *That really didn't matter to me*, they pretended, *I'll pick another one*. But some of us succeeded and went over the wall. My friend got a dance partner, learned his routine, and won first place in a state ballroom championship. I wrote and published my first book, *The Accountability Revolution*.

All these behaviors can happen. The question is: how do you walk yourself through the fear and do it anyway, while you are in it? Well, you focus on your bigger goal. You remember your intention. You become comfortable with the unknown. You reframe what scares you as what excites you. You acknowledge that you are afraid and you tell yourself: okay—we are going to do this anyway. You ask for support and encouragement. You write yourself a note card that says, "You can do it" and you carry it in your pocket. You let go of negative thinking. And always, no matter what you go through, action is the only real way out. One action, and another and another. Soon you are done with what seemed impossible to do. One small step at a time.

Taking Action Effectively

There are four strategies you can use to support efficient action. We will spend the remainder of this chapter exploring how to jump into action and step away from fear.

First: Take Small Steps

I was best man at my friend Martin's wedding. The morning of the big day, he got cold feet. He called me from his office and said he couldn't go through with the wedding. He said he was having an anxiety attack and his breathing seemed impaired. I suggested he forget all about the wedding and get in his car and go home. He could do that, right? Martin said he could, and I met him there. We broke the day into small actions: take a shower, put on the tuxedo, drive to the church, get out of the car. Gradually, Martin began to overcome his wedding-day jitters. Martin's small steps created a safety zone that enabled him to deal with the risks of change.

When your stretches are too long and your actions too big, you can easily outrun your safety zone. Whatever you're doing begins to feel like punishment because the actions are too scary. The answer is to scale down your actions. Create smaller actions that eliminate some of the pain. You still need to stretch beyond your comfort zone, but not so much that you will be paralyzed.

Practice is another way to build up your safety zone. Did you use a kickboard when you learned to swim or training wheels when you learned to ride a bike? Kickboards support beginning swimmers so they can practice kicking their legs without having to worry about sinking below the surface. Training wheels allow the new cyclist to gain a sense of balance while having the confidence of unquestionable support. Essentially, the kickboard and training wheels enlarge the safety zone.

Small steps are like incremental weight training. You can build your action muscles one step at a time. With each small step, you increase your knowledge and build trust in your own abilities. The stronger your muscles become, the more you can achieve with each new action you take. So, break your actions down into small steps. Don't try to change everything at once. Go for small changes and let success breed success!

Second: Keep Moving

The kinds of objectives that we are talking about in this book—major career, relationship, and personal achievements—require that you *move toward them.*

Momentum brings successes we tend to take for granted. I can't drive by a KFC restaurant without thinking of the chain's colorful founder, the Colonel himself, Harland Sanders. At age sixty-five, Sanders was forced into retirement when a new interstate highway bypassed his hotel and restaurant. After auctioning off the properties and paying the bills, his only income was a $105 monthly Social Security payment.

The one asset Sanders had left was a recipe for Kentucky Fried Chicken, and, as unlikely as this sounds, he spent the next two years on the road trying to secure some additional income by selling the right to make his chicken to restaurateurs across the country. Sanders later claimed he was turned down *more than 1,000 times* before he made a single sale. But he never quit moving toward his goal.

Five years after he started, two hundred restaurants were selling the Colonel's chicken. By 1964, more than six hundred restaurants had signed up. His retirement secured, Sanders sold his recipe and the franchise rights to a group of private investors for $2 million. Four decades later, more than two billion of the Colonel's chicken dinners have been sold—and you can buy them in eighty-two different countries.

It is pretty obvious that the Colonel (it's an honorary title, by the way) knew the secret of overcoming internal resistance. And now so do you. Keep moving; because if you stop, there is no way you will ever succeed.

Third: Use Your Support Network

We've talked about drawing on the support of others throughout this book, and nowhere is it more important than right now. Just as you can influence other people to act through your own efforts, so too can they influence you.

It is no coincidence that institutions that force us to face our toughest challenges often feature built-in support. If you look at addiction recovery programs such as Alcoholics Anonymous, you see that a major element is the use of *sponsors*: experienced members of AA who make themselves available on a face-to-face basis with new members. As new members struggle with their disease, they have someone to call on for advice and help. Often, that call makes all the difference between suppressing the need for a drink and falling off the wagon.

Another common form of support networks are the formal mentoring programs that so many organizations have adopted. Mentors help people to navigate careers and overcome barriers to success. For example, a hospital in the Midwest established a buddy system, in which managers from different departments were paired up to support each other. The manager of the operating room, who wasn't skilled in statistics and process improvement, was partnered with the manager of information technology, who was skilled in statistics but who didn't have a good understanding of the medical side of operations. They assisted each other in their own areas of expertise and exchanged knowledge. They met monthly and, based on a professional development plan, coached each other. Each manager was accountable for the success of both managers, so it was imperative that they support and coach each other. At the end of the year, an evaluation of each person was made and each was paired with another partner.

Similarly, the entire multilevel marketing industry utilizes the concept of support networks. Each salesperson recruits, trains, and supports the next level of representatives. In return, the recruiting member earns a commission on the sales of people that he or she has supported.

Does it work? Mary Kay Ash built the world's second largest direct seller of beauty products around the idea of ever-expanding levels of independent sales consultants supporting each other. Today, there are more than one million sales representatives selling Mary Kay cosmetics. Amway was built on the same concept. Its parent company, Alticor, Inc., neared $5 billion in annual sales, created by more than three million independent sales representatives who work for this consumer products direct marketer.

Without support, you are putting too much pressure on yourself to keep the ball rolling or to pick up the pieces when something breaks. Find people who you can call on to encourage you, push you, and egg you on. Reach out for help when you can't believe you have any chance at ever reaching your goal. You'll be amazed at what one person's belief in you can help you do.

Finally—and Most Importantly: Have a Recovery Plan

Recovery is the one strategy that is most often ignored. People work their way around the Personal Accountability Model and begin taking action without giving any thought to how they will react when things don't go according to plan. And let me tell you, things *will not* go according to plan.

The one thing you can count on when you start taking action is that you *will* get off-track. You will get discouraged about your progress, make mistakes, and slip back into old habits. That is why it is so critical that you develop and execute recovery plans.

Before you can recover, however, you need to measure your progress. When you take an action, you need to know if it is accomplishing the results that you anticipated. And, measurement is not just a number. You need to check to make sure your beliefs, emotions, and behaviors are supporting your goal. If you are on track, the measurement becomes a milestone to celebrate. But if you aren't, it is time to roll out your recovery plan.

RECOVERING OUR WAY TO THE MOON

In May 1961, President John Kennedy stood before Congress and declared a national goal: the United States would send a man to the moon within the decade. It was not exactly unthinkable, but the country's longest space flight at that time had only been a 115-mile high, partial earth orbit. The 250,000-mile trip to the moon was surely a stretch.

NASA met Kennedy's challenge on July 20, 1969, when Apollo 11 landed on the moon and Neil Armstrong and Buzz Aldrin took their historic steps on the lunar surface. But, the decade-long process of reaching that goal was hardly defect-free. If you study the story of that great venture, you become struck by how many things went wrong while NASA made efforts to land on the moon. In fact, not a single flight was perfect. Any honest assessment would conclude that we *recovered* our way to the moon.

NASA's ability to recover from unexpected failures like the tragedy of Apollo 1 proved to be its greatest asset. Rather than abort any future missions into space, NASA learned from the terrible tragedy of Apollo 1, when a fire in the capsule killed three astronauts on the landing pad during a routine exercise. They also learned from the defective indicator lights that almost caused them to abort the final descent to the moon's surface.

In fact, recovery was built into every aspect of the Apollo effort. The astronauts and their backup crews literally spent tens of thousands of hours in simulators. NASA created, staffed, and maintained an entire organization devoted to throwing every possible scenario at the crews. And over and over, the efforts paid off as things went wrong and were quickly noted, analyzed, and corrected.

The most dramatic example of recovery was the Apollo 13 mission, which Ron Howard recounted in the film of the same name. Watch that film when you get a chance, and focus on how both the astronauts and Mission Control respond to the mid-flight explosion that blew the side off of the spacecraft. It is among the most amazing feats of recovery you will ever see.

Recovery Begins With Recommitment

Look back at your intention and revisit your goal. Make sure you are still committed to both your intention and your goal. And then, forgive yourself for getting off-track so you don't fall into victim behaviors and blame or judge yourself.

The next task is to reexamine your action. Ask yourself what didn't work. Do you simply need to resume the action and execute it more effectively, or is there something you need to do differently? Sometimes you will just start over. You might need to pick a different action altogether. When you know which action is required of you, take that action. Then take another action and another until you reach your goal.

The lesson to remember is that you don't achieve your goals because you're perfect. You *can* achieve them if you use your ability to correct course and recover from your mistakes. Plan what you will do when you get off-course, put that plan to work if you do, then marvel at how you sustained the rocky course and reached your goal anyway.

Take small steps, keep moving, use your support network, and have a recovery plan. If you do those four things, you will hit your mark. Then what? What should you do when you achieve a desired outcome?

The natural reflex is to move on to the next one but we invite you to add a step. A small or a huge one. Depending on your style and the magnitude of what you accomplished. Take time to celebrate. Acknowledge yourself and those who have helped you. Fill up your bank of support. Fill up theirs. It prepares everybody for the next challenge. Read on and explore this concept further in the conclusion.

| Exercise | **TAKE ACTION NOW** |

Step 1: Clarify your actions

Based on your intentions, goals, and lessons learned from previous chapters, identify three actions you can take to move forward on accomplishing your dreams. Keep the actions small to ensure success.

Step 2: Solidify your commitment

For each action, commit to a start date and a target date for completion. Getting started is the most important step to being successful.

Step 3: Identify your support system

Make a list of the people, environmental conditions, or tools that will support you in taking action. This could include a friend or coworker, playing music or lighting a candle in your office, or making sure you have canvasses for painting.

Step 4: Create a recovery plan

Identify anything that could cause you to get off-track. Maybe you get delayed from starting or you run into difficulties completing your first action. What will you do to recover and get back on-track? What is your contingency plan? This is a key step in maintaining your momentum when obstacles are out of your control.

Step 5: Celebrate success

Success is not only determined after you complete your goal. Success is recognized and celebrated after each action you complete that moves you toward your goal. Even if it takes you off-course, celebrate the learning you get from the experience. It is all preparation for achieving and sustaining success.

CONCLUSION

The gift of accountability. *The root of the word accountability is "counting on". Counting on others and mostly counting on ourselves. Are we going to have the courage to recognize what doesn't work, own the role we played in the making of this situation, forgive ourselves and others for what we judged in the process? Are we going to have what it takes to examine ourselves, learn new behaviors, and move into a different action? Well, we think yes. We think that it is worth it. We think that the stakes are so high, it will be worth every minute you invest in yourself.*

The Gift of Accountability

Celebrate Every Moment of Every Day

My wife and I were having dinner a while ago in a nice restaurant. The waiter came over at the beginning of our meal to ask if we would be ordering dessert. He said we should choose before the meal, not only because it required thirty minutes to cook but mostly because we would be eating our meal differently if we chose how it was going to end. He said we would enjoy each bite of the appetizers and entrées as if it were a journey toward such a wonderful destination. Like life—I thought to myself. If I can choose the ending, I can enjoy each moment that leads me there.

This book ends with dessert. It ends with the idea that celebration is the dessert of every day. How can you end your life, your meal, your project, every moment of every day *celebrating* because it is full of what mattered to you? How would you like to lie in bed most nights knowing that this day could make the list of your favorite days? The short list. Every day. Not so much because of what happened but because of what you *did* with what happened.

Celebrating is an essential part of success. You actually can't fully move on if you don't take a moment to acknowledge the road traveled. That is why movie crews have wrap parties: to complete, to close the loop of achievement, to allow them to conclude what just happened, and also to gear up for the next project.

Sadly, this step is often neglected. It is strange how we tend to be more familiar with the sense that we are not enough, that we should have done this better or faster. It is easier to see where we fell short than it is to see when we did a really good job.

The Risk of Not Celebrating

"We don't have time to stop and acknowledge success." "Why should I recognize your effort when you are just doing your job?" "My kids will be arrogant if I start telling them how great they are." "If I pat myself on the back, I will get lazy." These are the excuses we commonly hear when we talk about the lack of celebration. *Sharing appreciation* and *acknowledging success* are necessary for getting closure. Celebration is necessary to build self-esteem. It is necessary to move on to the next goal without holding on to the previous one. It doesn't take much time; it takes no money. It is inspiring, supportive. It is kind to yourself and the ones around you. It makes people want to give the best they have. It is a simple way of saying thank you. It is a profound way for people to know that they have done something meaningful. And that goes for you, too.

Yes, the opposite is true. Not celebrating, not supporting, not acknowledging stops you from your next success. It will eventually deplete your energy and your enthusiasm.

Have an Attitude of Gratitude

Be grateful you had what it took to succeed and be thankful for the help you received in the process. Challenge yourself to find a reason to be thankful—for you and others. Maybe you had a creative idea. Maybe your kid cleaned up without you needing to beg. Or maybe you completed a difficult project on time. Maybe your colleague landed a new account. Maybe you asked for help and allowed someone to contribute to your success. Or you made a healthy choice at lunch. Maybe you realized your mom taught you the value of integrity. Or you listened compassionately and made a great difference to a friend. Whatever it is you did, pat yourself on the back. Pat them on the back. Start building your emotional bank account. And theirs. Then the next time you have to tackle a big project or life challenges you, you can draw on this wealth of inner support and acknowledgment. And you will be more confident and trusting that you are able to accomplish the task at hand. And so will the people around you.

Renew Your Intention

Now that you have celebrated, you can move on to the final and never-ending step. Choose what you are going to do next, or learn next, or be next. Recommit. What is the next thing that matters to you? My friend David Allen, whom I mentioned before, suggests keeping a running list that he calls "some day maybe." He recommends *capturing* what you want to accomplish, even if you are not yet ready to put any energy into it. Being a scratch golfer, learning sign language, swimming with dolphins, building a dream house, meeting Stevie Wonder, reading stories at a children's shelter, learning to play piano—these are all some of mine. When I am done with one project, I visit that list and I choose my next adventure. That way, I not only accomplish what I have to, but also what I *want* to do.

It's Not About Perfection

This book is not about perfection. It's about the opposite of perfection. An accountable life is full of failures—but they are failures followed by *forgiveness*, *learning*, and *understanding*. Use your failures as steppingstones for your next level of competence. You can't anticipate all the situations that are going to come at you: life is too creative. The process we have identified in this book allows you to bounce back and switch from the *unsupportive* Victim Loop to a more constructive approach—the *accountable* approach.

Enjoy Your Journey

As we have explored in this book, when you are faced with a situation, you have choices. You can choose to ignore, deny, blame, rationalize, resist, hide, and spiral down in a Victim Loop that literally has no bottom. It keeps on going down. Or you can choose to recognize, own, forgive, self-examine, learn, and take action. That spiral takes you up. That spiral gives you the ticket to a fulfilling life that you would be excited to share when you are sitting on a bench somewhere looking back at your life.

INDEX

ACKNOWLEDGMENTS

Writing a book, very much like building our own character, takes the dedication of many people. Each individual listed here has contributed to shaping us and, in many ways, shaping this book. As you read through our acknowledgments, we invite you to think of the people who have inspired you, those who have helped you be your very best.

In this spirit of deep appreciation, we would like to thank

Our children, Sarah and Leah, who teach us every day the meaning of loving in the moment; Danny Miller, Kendall Hailey and Nancy Grossman for sharing the parenting adventure with us.

Our families, Martine and Claude Chiche; Laurent and Alexa Chiche; Francine and Philippe Siliart; Anny and Jean Fort; Kareen Trager-Lewis; Benjamin and Thomas Michel; Pascale Trager-Lewis; Christian and Emma Chevalier; Jacques and Jacqueline Laloum; Brigitte, Alain, Sarah, Nathaniel, and Raphael Werteimer; Frederic Laloum; Helyett Zerbib; Alain and Jonathan Zerbib; Chantal, Serge, Lisa, and Leo Goldstein; Erroll, Lydia and Simon Cohen; Fréderic Chiche; Davee Gunn; Virginia Burt; Sandi, Paul, Adam, and Mitch Caplan; Hannah, Robyn, and Steve State; Gloria, Barry, Fern, Michael, and Fran Krugel; Brenda and Stephen Stein.

Our staff members and business associates, without whom our business would not be possible, nor would it be nearly as enjoyable: Todd Alexander; Veronica Alweiss; Nancy Bendik; Patricia and Thane Bertoli-Berti; Valerie Bishop; Leslie Boyer; Hal Brand; David Bransky; John Brogan; Matt Byerts; Patrick Carroll; Jennifer Cayer; John Clark; Peter Cope; Cynthia David; Dottie DeHart; Teresa Edmondson; Jonathan Ellerby; Don Formiller; Jane Grossman; Isabel Hernandez; Ami Irwin; Greg Irwin; Chris Johnen; Carole Kammen; Ted Kinni; Geri Lopker; Rob Mello; Marcia McCready; Sky Moreno; Deanna Morton; Nicole

Paige; Guy Paproski; Joan Pastor, Ph.D.; Michelle Rochwarger; Mark Sankey; Robert Simkins; Leslie Smith; Kit Stetina; Connie Stomper, Ph.D; Marianne Thompson; Barbara Thrasher; David Vered; Jamie Woolf; Jonathan Wygant; Nancy Young, Ph.D.; and Andrea Zuckerman.

The generous spirits that have contributed their much appreciated support, by way of an endorsement: Joseph P. Allen; Ernie Banks; Heide Banks; Dr. Robert L. Barber; Ken Blanchard; Robert J. Byerts, Jr.; Christina R. Campbell; Adam Clark; Elizabeth Forsythe Hailey; Kirk Froggatt; Arianna Huffington; Lt. David Kain, FDNY, Ret.; Loral Langemeier; Perry J. Ludy; James T. Lussier; Dr. Mary E.F. McInerney; Dr. John W. McCredie; Rabbi Levi Meier, Ph.D.; James W. Montgomery; Olivia; Vic Parrish; Dr. Brian Postl; Celia Rocks; Stu Semigran; Anthony E. Shaw; Gene D. Thin Elk; Terry Tillman; Paul Trinidad; David Williams; and Larry M. Zucker, L.C.S.W.

Our friends, coaches and mentors: Stéphane Akoun; David and Kathryn Allen; Brigitte Antoine; Gérard Apfeldorfer; Val Austin-Wiebe; Francoise Bavcevic; Jacques Becker; Beverly Berg; Helen and Allan Bradley; Caroline Braun; Peter Braun; Laren Bright; Janet and Lawrence Caminite; Aude Cardinal; Patrick Carmichael; Willie Carmichael; Vanessa Chauvin; Steve Chopyak, D.C.; Kerry, Meggie and H.C. "Chip" Clitheroe, Jr., Ph.D.; Paul Crane, M.D.; Simon Croué; Olivier Dassault; Martine Desmoulins; Robert DiNunzio; Vincent and Marilyn Dupont; Patrice Ellequain; Bernice Evans-Mazique; Monique Fabre; Kent Falk; Patrick, Rolande and Morgan Fellous; Philippe Feyeux; Rose-Marie, Dominique, Sarah, and Penelope Fournier; Rama Fox; Emile Frydlender; Norm Frye; Randy Garver; Marc Germes; Marie-Jeanne Godard; Monique Godard; Alain Godet; Charles Golden; Judi Golfader; Feli di Gorgio; Mark Goodman, MD; Eric Grabli; Nancy Greystone; Sherry and Ivan Grossman, M.D.; Steve Grossman; Mimine Gruyer; Jessie Guigliano; Frank Guillon; Michael Hayes; Amir Hegazi; Mark and Rose Hennings; Margot and Robert Hillman, Ph.D; Laura Hillman; Dan Ho; Drs. Ron and Mary Hulnick; Stéphane Jardin; Daniel Jibert; Sharon Kagan; Varda Kakon; Paul Kaye; Mahan Jiwan Kaur and Singh Khalsa; Chantal Kelly; Peter Knight-Meyers; Barre Lando; Kim Langbecker; Emma Ledoyen; Naomi Lieberman M.A. M.F.T; Alcene Looper; Sarah and Victor Levy; Mark Lurie; Ofelia Mancera;

Anna and Chou Mangeard; Gregg McHatton; Leila Nichols; Alexia Norton; Ann Otis; Alain Pewzner; Véronique Philbois; Todd Pierce; Doug Preston; Sue Pushkar; Tracy Quinton; Bob Ricioli; David and Teresa Rodgers; Teresa Roche, Ph.D; Arnaud de Saint-Simon; Mike Sanders; Harry Saperstein, M.D.; Judy Seabridge; Stéphanie Semonin; Pascale Senk; Jean-Louis Servan Schreiber; Brian Sholder, D.D.S.; Steve Shull; Fleur, Florent and Angelo Siri; Agapi Stassinopoulos; Tim Souris; Anna Souza; Tim Stalder; Gary Stewart; Claudia Thair; Lynn Timermann; Charles Toney; Anne and Bernard Tormo; Gabrielle Tormo; Pascal Turbil; Lois and Paul Vallerga; Patrice Van Erseel; Mathilde and Timothé Vitry; Matthieu Wallaert; Agnes, Laurence, Gilbert and Bledina Weil; Gad Weil; Samuel Zaoui; Zelia; Izak Zenou and Jean-Philippe Zermati.

Writing a book can be the most exciting or the most grueling experience. Working so closely with our publisher turned friend made this adventure one of our favorite ever. We will never forget how a single individual could change our world so dramatically. You are one of the grandest thinkers of this time. And that goes for your team: Ruth, Sherry, and Tom, thank you. It may have been said in every printed book, but it is so true: we could not have done it without you.

And to you, the reader, we want to give thanks for choosing this book, giving us your time so generously, and trusting that you will get something in return. Our wish for you is that our words inspire you to see a situation with a different perspective, possibly make a different choice, and as a result-feel better about yourself, your life, your world.

Mark: Soph, thank you for writing this book with me. You have taken complicated concepts and turned them into an easy guide to follow. You have translated corporate lingo into a book that I am proud to send to all the people I know. Thank you.

Sophie: Mark, your insights are changing the way people think. They are realizing the power they have to make their lives a better place to live in. It has been an honor to serve as the scribe of many of your concepts. I would do it again and again.

ABOUT IMPAQ

In business since 1978, IMPAQ pioneered the accountability movement, and is now an international management consulting and training firm recognized for its research, publishing, and methodologies in helping clients build individual and organizational accountability. IMPAQ teams with Fortune 500 companies, healthcare organizations, government agencies, and nonprofit foundations worldwide, setting new standards of excellence and achieving improved performance and business results.

ACCOUNTABILITY SERVICES AND PRODUCTS

IMPAQ offers a variety of programs foundational for creating a work environment dedicated to accountable performance and team relationships. IMPAQ also offers products that support individuals and teams in maximizing their accountability experience

For more information on IMPAQ's services and products, please visit www.IMPAQcorp.com or call (800) 332-2251.

THE CENTER FOR PEACEFUL ACCOUNTABILITY

Peaceful Accountability is peace in action. The Center For Peaceful Accountability is a nonprofit foundation dedicated to bringing accountable principles and practices into communities and families in order to raise quality of life. Schools, prisons, charitable organizations, and unique communities create an accountable environment based on integrity, cooperation, and action; an environment in which personal transformation is experienced, success is achieved, and results are measured.

As individuals thrive within their community or team, they become accountable leaders dedicated to the betterment of themselves and their communities. The result is greater peace in action.

For more information on IMPAQ's services and products, please visit www.IMPAQcorp.com or call (800) 332-2251

ACCOUNTABILITY GET-TOGETHERS TOOL KIT

If you are interested in starting an Accountability Get-Together at the office with your team or at home with your family or friends, you can purchase a starter kit that will give you everything you need (but the tea and cookies) to lead fun, supportive, transformational meetings and gatherings.

Following the teachings of this book, you will have an opportunity to coach yourself and one another to take the learnings to the next level.

In the kit, you will receive fun games, creative activities, suggested topics of conversations, a poster to hang in your meetings, and other tools to sustain you in implementing what you have read in this book.

For more information and to order, send an e-mail to gettogether@impaqcorp.com

ACCOUNTABILITY TELECONFERENCE

Join our eight-week series teleconference facilitated by Mark and Sophie. Each weekly one-hour session explores in detail each topic of the book. Be a part of this nationwide conversation. Deepen what you have read and receive individual coaching from the comfort of your home. More importantly—achieve what matters to you.

For more information and to sign up, send an e-mail to teleconference@impaqcorp.com

ACCOUNTABILITY RETREATS

Come with us on a retreat and be guided through a dynamic journey of self-exploration revealing insights into your own power of personal accountability. We will take you to inspirational destinations and return you home invigorated and equipped with new personal insights and skills to enrich your professional and personal development. The format is a balance of rejuvenation, experience, and study, facilitated by a unique team of experts in the fields of health, relationships, finances, time management, leadership, and organization.

For more information and to register, send an e-mail to retreat@impaqcorp.com

ABOUT THE AUTHORS

Mark Samuel is the president and founder of IMPAQ, a worldwide consulting firm focusing on individual and business accountability, and the nationally acclaimed author of *The Accountability Revolution, Achieving Breakthrough Results in Half the Time!* He has been featured in *Fortune Magazine* as a top authority on "how  companies can end blame in the ranks, and create a place where people want to work and get results" and has appeared on Bloomberg and CNBC.

Considered a practical visionary by Fortune 500 companies, Mark teaches organizations how to thrive in the competitive twenty-first century global marketplace through results-oriented management based upon the practice of accountability.

As an award-winning speaker, Mark has been guiding organizations worldwide to higher levels of sustainable success through his innovative accountability-based programs for twenty-two years. Mark holds a Bachelor's Degree in Social Science, a Master's Degree in Management, with a special emphasis in Organizational Development and a Master's Degree in Applied Psychology.

Sophie Chiche is the chief operating officer of IMPAQ, and is firmly committed to the principles of personal and team accountability. She also acts as the creative advisor for the development of IMPAQ's image, drawing from her diverse and highly accomplished artistic background.

Before joining IMPAQ, Sophie served as the U.S. correspondent for the European publication, *Psychologies Magazine*, writing primarily about the human potential movement, and she continues to speak passionately and eloquently on the subject. Her ability to capture the essence of personal accountability and relay it to her audience is unsurpassed. Sophie holds a Bachelor of Arts Degree in Business and a Master's Degree in Applied Psychology.